A Critical Thinker's Guide
To Educational Fads

Contents

Introduction

The history of education is also the history of educational panaceas, the comings and goings of quick fixes for deep-seated educational problems. This old problem is dramatically on the increase. The result is intensifying fragmentation of energy and effort in the schools, together with a significant waste of time and money. Many teachers become increasingly cynical and jaded.

It is time to recognize that education will never be improved by educational fads, and that the manner in which educational trends are marketed guarantees that they will be transformed into fads. Fads by their nature are fated to self-destruction. Parents, educators, and citizen activists need to understand the problem of educational fads so that they can effectively distinguish substantive efforts at educational reform from superficial ones. Hence the motivation for this guide.

By "fad" we mean an idea that is embraced enthusiastically for a short time. In schooling, this typically means a short-lived emphasis on a seemingly wonderful new idea that will transform teaching and learning without much effort on anyone's part. Since by definition a fad will quickly come and go, it cannot be expected to improve instruction in any significant way. By "trend" we mean a general tendency or movement in a certain direction. Trends in schooling typically last 7-10 years, but may last longer.

Included in the sidebar on this page is an incomplete list of some of the educational trends or fads on the market today. Each has ideological advocates. Each must be critically assessed for theoretical

Educational Fads

Alignment
Assessment
Authentic Pedagogy
  & Assessment
Block Scheduling
Bloom's Taxonomy
Brain-Based Teaching
  & Learning
Character Education
Charter Schools
Choice *(Vouchers & Privatization)*
Constructivism
Cooperative Learning
Core Knowledge
Creative Thinking
Critical Thinking
Cultural Literacy
Didactic Teaching
Emotional Intelligence
Feminism and Gender Issues
Gifted Education
Global Education
Inquiry-Based Learning
Integrated Curriculum
Intelligence
Learning Styles
Multiculturalism
Multiple Intelligences
No Child Left Behind
Outcome-Based Education
Phonics vs. Whole Language
Portfolio-Based Assessment
Problem Solving
"Raise the Standards"
  Movement
Restructuring Schools
  Movement
School-Based Management
School Choice
School-To-Work Movement
Self-Esteem Movement
Socratic Questioning
Teaching for Understanding
Thematic Curriculum

underpinnings and proper application. Note: For some of the fads or trends in this guide, we mean "an emphasis on…," as in "assessment," "intelligence," and so forth. This should be clear as you read through the list.

To these may be added a variety of programs focused on drug abuse prevention, child abuse prevention, sex education, extracurricular activities, school improvement, gang control, violence prevention, hunger and malnutrition, mainstreaming, individualized education, special education of differing varieties, dropout prevention and at-risk, and so forth. The list is seemingly endless.

Educational Fads

Most educational trends or fads originate in reasonable ideas. All reasonable ideas about education enhance instruction when integrated into a substantive concept of education. They fail when imposed upon instruction through a non-substantive, fragmented conception of education, which is unfortunately typically the case in schooling today. In this guide, we briefly critique many of the current educational trends and fads.

Our goal is to make the basic idea behind each of these fads intelligible so that its proper use — and likely misuse — can be taken into account. It is our aim to provide the reader with key questions to be raised in discussing these ideas. Each trend or fad is commented upon in three ways:

- the essential idea behind the trend or fad,
- the proper educational use (when integrated into a substantive concept of education), and
- the likely misuse (when the idea is unreasonably applied).

It is not our goal to provide a full and complete explication of any of these. In general, we recommend the Phi Delta Kappan for more detailed articles on virtually all of these trends or fads. This journal is readily available through most public libraries. Our goal is to provide a foundation which can be used to put all educational trends/fads into immediate perspective, making it possible for interested persons to grasp the essential idea and understand the potential use and misuse of that idea. With these understandings one can make sense of discussions of educational reform issues. One can then formulate the relevant and substantial questions and seek the answers one deserves.

We provide the "essential idea" so the reader will understand the basic thinking behind this trend or fad. We provide the "educational use" so the reader will understand how the idea may legitimately be used or taken into account in instruction. We provide the "misuse" so the reader may be on the lookout for its inappropriate (and often most likely) use.

Most people are overwhelmed by the sheer mass of educational fads. Most educators feel pulled in a variety of directions by them. Some become passionate devotees of one of the fads at the expense of substantive education. And virtually all educational trends with any substance are transformed into fads by a flawed or superficial understanding of the basic idea behind the trend combined with a non-substantive concept of education to begin with.

We need to get off the educational fad roller coaster altogether. We can do this if we take a substantive concept of critical thinking seriously for the first time in our educational history. To get off the educational fad roller coaster is to refuse to conceive of any idea as a cure-all. It is to treat all ideas as elements subordinate to a substantive concept of education.

Substantive and Non-Substantive Concepts of Education

By a substantive concept of education we mean one that highlights the essential components of education, consequently one that has clear implications for how we should understand "the educated person" and how we should design the educational process. Many popular concepts of education are non-substantive in that they are vague and fragmented, and therefore superficial and misleading. They do not highlight the common dimensions of the various disciplines. They do not illuminate essential intellectual standards. They do not define essential intellectual traits (the personal characteristics that, when acquired, direct the right use of the mind). Instead, they lead to instruction that mainly trains, indoctrinates, or socializes rather than educates the individual. They produce "counterfeits" of educated persons because they ignore essential abilities, standards, and traits in the instructional process.

A Substantive Concept of Education
(*The Educated Person*)

Standards and Abilities

Educated persons share common intellectual standards and abilities. An educated person values and seeks to achieve clarity, accuracy, precision, relevance, depth, breadth, logicalness, and significance in thinking. Conversely, no person can be said to be educated whose thinking is characteristically unclear, imprecise, inaccurate, irrelevant, superficial, narrow-minded, illogical, or insignificant.

Similarly, an educated person masters the elements that underlie and define the structure of all thought:

- An educated person routinely seeks to identify key purposes and goals and explicitly formulates questions, problems, and issues necessary to accomplishing those purposes and goals.
- An educated person gathers relevant information and makes reasonable inferences from that information (in tackling questions, problems and issues they are seeking to answer, solve, or resolve).
- An educated person notices key assumptions (that underlie thinking) and important implications and consequences (that follow from thinking).
- An educated person effectively analyzes key concepts and recognizes points of view and is able to shift either or both when necessary (in attempting to solve a problem or resolve an issue).

Intellectual Traits and Values

An educated person demonstrates intellectual humility, intellectual honesty, intellectual autonomy, intellectual integrity, intellectual perseverance, intellectual empathy, and fair-mindedness in thought, work, and in every part of life. These characteristics are the essential foundations for the right use of the mind. Lacking these characteristics, humans think and act egocentrically, do not respect reason and evidence (except when it is in their selfish interest to do so), and are indifferent to the welfare of others (with whom they do not egocentrically identify).

These intellectual standards, abilities, traits, and values — integrated — define the educated person. Without them one is unable to internalize the logic of academic content or reason effectively or fair-mindedly about problems and decisions in everyday life.

A Substantive Concept of Education
(*The Educational Process*)

A substantive concept of education not only highlights the qualities of the educated person, but also implies the proper design of the educational process. There are essential minimal conditions for cultivating educated minds. These entail modes of instruction that facilitate development of the standards, abilities, and traits of the educated person. All of the traditional content areas of school may be, but typically are not, taught so as to conduce to those standards, abilities, and traits.

For example, when history is substantively taught, it is taught as historical thinking, the major goal: to give students practice in thinking historically (analyzing, evaluating, and reconstructing historical interpretations and problems). As a result, students learn not only how to read historical texts with insight and understanding, but also how to gather important facts and write well developed historical essays of their own. Through this mode of instruction, students come to see the significance of historical thinking both in their own lives and in the life of culture and society. History becomes — in such a transformed mind, — not random facts from the past, but a way to reason about the past to make intelligent decisions in the present and reasonable plans for the future.

When science is substantively taught, it is taught as scientific thinking, the major goal: to give students practice in thinking scientifically. As a result, students learn not only how to read science texts with insight and understanding, but also how to formulate plausible scientific hypotheses, make reasonable scientific predictions, design scientific experiments, gather facts scientifically and make justifiable scientific inferences based on the facts gathered. When this is done effectively students come to see the significance of scientific thinking both in their own lives and in the life of culture and society. In such a transformed mind, science becomes, not random technical facts and theories to be memorized, but a way to reason about the world to understand its systemic functions and the ways its laws can be used for the welfare of persons and the biosphere.

When mathematics is substantively taught, it is taught as mathematical thinking, the major goal: to give students practice in thinking mathematically. As a result, students learn not only how to read math texts with insight and understanding, but also how to formulate and analyze mathematical problems, and how to reason from the information stated in those problems to solutions (which they are able to explain and test). When this is effectively done, students come to see the significance of mathematical thinking both in their own lives and in the life of culture and society. In such a transformed mind, mathematics becomes not random facts about numbers and spatial objects to be memorized for a test, but a way to reason about the quantitative dimensions of the world, a precisely-defined set of ideas and insights that can be used for the welfare of persons and the biosphere.

When literature is substantively taught, it is taught as literary thinking. The major goal: to give students practice in thinking analytically and critically about literary texts. As a result, students learn not only how to read novels, plays, short stories, and poems with insight, understanding, and appreciation, but also how to formulate and analyze literary problems, reasoning from information in a literary text to plausible interpretations and judgments of appreciation (which they are able to explain and defend on reasonable grounds). When this is effectively done, students come to see the significance of literature, literary thinking, and imagination both in their own lives and in the life of culture and society. Literature becomes an important way to learn about human nature and the human condition as well as a lifelong source of insight and pleasure.

When students are taught using a substantive concept of education as the guide to the design of instruction, they learn to initiate, analyze, and evaluate their own thinking and the thinking of others (within all the content areas they study). Doing so, they come to act more reasonably and effectively in every part of life. They are able to do this because they have acquired intellectual tools and intellectual standards essential to sound reasoning and personal and professional judgment. Self-assessment becomes an integral part of their lives. They are able to master content in diverse disciplines. They become proficient readers, writers, speakers, and listeners. They use their learning to raise the quality of their lives and the lives of others. They become reasonable and fair-minded persons capable of empathizing with views with which they disagree and disagreeing with views uncritically accepted by those around them. They are able to use their reasoning skills to contribute to their own emotional life and transform their desires and motivations accordingly. They come to think, feel, and act effectively and with integrity.

"Fixing" Schools Superficially

There are no panaceas in education. There is no one simple way to fix the schools. To fix the schools we must fix the thinking that is running the schools. We must persuade those whose thinking is running schools to adopt a substantive concept of education.

But there are a variety of persons whose thinking is running the schools, and we can directly control only one person's thinking, our own. So even if we are part of the process and our thinking is influencing what is happening in school, there are always a variety of others whose thinking is bound to impact the quality of learning. This is what makes the problem vexing and unlikely to be solved in the short run. Consider the variety of those whose thinking is clearly involved.

The Thinking of Administrators

Few administrators have a substantive concept of education. Very often the thinking of administrators is focused on troubleshooting short-range problems, handling complaints, settling disputes, and making sure that legal and bureaucratic requirements are met. Typically, concepts of education, substantive or otherwise, seem an insignificant abstraction unrelated to their day-to-day problems. At the same time, the thinking of key administrators shapes decisions which have immediate and long-range consequences on teaching and learning. They make decisions which significantly impact the design of inservice programs, the curriculum, and the evaluation of teaching and learning. Their leadership, or lack thereof, determines whether a substantive concept of education ever becomes the subject of discussion, not to mention whether it is ever taken seriously, by parents, teachers, or school board. With regard to inservice programs, administrators often find it politically expedient to provide a variety of choices from an array of fads popular with different groups of teachers. Rarely is there integration between these programs. Virtually never are presenters required to integrate their recommendations into a substantive conception of education.

The Thinking of Teachers

Few teachers have a substantive concept of education. Very often teachers are focused on day-to-day survival, getting lessons prepared, avoiding local politics, fitting into the system, incorporating the latest fad into their classes (often at the direction of administrators on some new fad bandwagon), and attempting to fulfill curriculum requirements. Covering bodies of content often drives instruction, with masses of papers to grade and other requirements to be met. Immediate, short-range imperatives seem (to them) to dominate their lives. Thinking about the long-term and about a substantive concept of education often seems to them like "pie in the sky" — abstract, theoretical, and unrealistic.

The Thinking of Students

The thinking of students produces a positive or negative response to their teachers, fellow students, and the content to be learned. Very few students have a substantive concept of education. Most think of the schools either as a place to socialize and have fun or a place to be passively tolerated. Most students have never heard a discussion in class about what education is, and hence about what one should strive to achieve in learning, and why. Until students develop a substantive concept of education they are not likely to actively cooperate in developing standards, abilities, and traits essential to the educated mind.

The Thinking of Parents

The thinking of parents shapes decisions in the parenting process, which, in turn, has significant implications for the attitudes and understandings that students bring into the classroom. Unfortunately, few parents have a substantive concept of education. Some even press for the memorization of masses of content since that is what they did as a student (and they assume that they were educated thereby). Or they are primarily concerned with their children's grades and test scores, pressing them to perform well in order to graduate from high school, go to college, or attend a prestigious university. Rarely do parents have a clear (not to mention deep) concept of the educated person.

The Thinking of School Board Members

The thinking of the school board members results in long-range school goals and decisions, and the broad policies to be followed in pursuing those goals. Yet few board members have a substantive concept of education. Few have the intellectual tools for formulating a reasonable idea of the educated person. Few are themselves engaged in lifelong learning.

The Thinking of Legislators and Governors

The thinking of legislators and governors creates public policy and determines levels and kinds of financial support for schools and instructional programs. Most assume that they understand exactly what the schools need. Though, if truth were told, few have a substantive concept of education.

The Thinking of Activist Citizens

The thinking of activist citizens challenges, pressures, modifies, redirects, or reinforces the status quo in the schools. Nevertheless, few activists have a substantive concept of education, though many sense that there is something fundamentally wrong with the schools.

Fixing the Schools
(Substantively)

Non-substantive thinking at any level is bound to have a negative effect on education. The tragedy is that as a culture, we have yet to learn to take responsibility for the superficiality of our thinking. We think, but we do not know how we think. We think, but we are unable to take our thinking apart. We think, but we do not understand the standards and criteria we are using as we think. We think, but we do not know how to adjust our thinking to the nature of the problem or question we are thinking about. Put most simply, we think, but we generally don't think in such a way as to grasp the problems we are facing non-superficially.

If there is a single answer to human problems, disciplined, reflective, substantive thinking is that answer. But everyone must develop disciplined reasoning abilities for themselves. Everyone must cultivate the skills and dispositions of the critical mind within their minds, using their own thinking. We cannot get into your head and fix your thinking. We cannot forcibly change your view of your thinking or of what is wrong or right with the schools. We cannot even force you to take your own thinking seriously or to pay more attention to it. And you, in turn, are in the same circumstance in relation to others. You cannot get into the head of someone else and fix their thinking. Administrators who think well and have a substantive concept of education cannot implant that concept in the heads of other administrators, nor in the heads of teachers and parents. Teachers who have a substantive concept of education cannot implant that concept in the heads of other teachers, nor of their students. One person can influence another, finally, only with the cooperation of that other. And from the inside of your own mind, your own thinking usually appears to be damned good, and not really in need of changing. (In other words, if everyone thought like you, the world would be a pretty fine place, right?)

What follows, then, is a brief summary of educational trends and fads for your consideration. Our goal is to persuade you that there are no "magic bullets" for the schools. The only reasonable solution to raising the quality of education is in-depth thinking based on a substantive concept of education. This developed concept is the basis for incorporating reasonable ideas for school improvement while avoiding the fragmentation and faddishness that usually results. Superficial, fragmented thinking continually backfires on us, undermines our future, distorts our past, and wastes the opportunities of the present.

Disciplined, substantive thinking at the heart of educational reform offers the best hope for long-term success. We will demonstrate its power and necessity by using it to systematically review and assess many current educational trends and fads. By systematically developing our own thinking and by systematically encouraging, stimulating, and rewarding the in-depth thinking of others, we do all that we can to improve the quality of the schools.

Now, before we begin our commentary on each individual trend or fad, we will do two things. First, we will summarize the essential learning requirements (in attaining a substantive education) under three categories: skills and abilities, intellectual standards & traits, and modes of thinking. Second, we will suggest questions that should be asked of every reform enthusiast, independent of the trend or fad they may be advocating.

Attaining Substantive Education[1]

Skills and Abilities Essential to Learning Across the Curriculum

The student understands and effectively uses the elements that underlie the structure of all thinking in all domains of human thought.[1]

To meet this requirement, the student will:

- accurately identify key purposes and goals and explicitly formulate

1   For an overview of the conceptual underpinnings of critical thinking, see the appendix.

questions, problems, and issues requisite to accomplishing those purposes and goals in mastering subject matter and content.

- effectively gather relevant information and data and make reasonable inferences from that information (in seeking to answer, solve, or resolve questions, problems or issues) in mastering subject matter and content.

- notice key assumptions (that underlie thinking) and important implications and consequences (that follow from thinking) in mastering subject matter and content.

- effectively analyze key concepts and ideas, recognize relevant points of view, and shift one's concepts or viewpoint when necessary (in attempting to solve a problem or resolve an issue) in mastering subject matter and content.

Intellectual Standards Essential to Learning Across the Curriculum

The student understands and effectively uses interdisciplinary intellectual criteria essential to sound thinking.

To meet this requirement, the student will assess thinking:

- for its clarity (effectively determining whether it is well-stated, elaborated, illustrated, and exemplified).

- for its accuracy (effectively determining whether it is free from errors, mistakes, or distortion).

- for its precision (effectively determining whether it is in need of further specification and exactness)

- for its relevance (effectively determining whether it bears on the matter at hand or question at issue).

- for its depth (effectively determining whether it deals adequately with the complexity of the matter at hand or question at issue).

- for its breadth (effectively determining whether it deals adequately with important alternative points of view).

- for its logicalness (effectively determining whether it makes sense and is consistent).

- for its significance (effectively determining whether and to what extent it deals with questions, problems, or issues of importance — as against those that are trivial or peripheral).

- for its fairness (effectively determining whether it takes into account the views of relevant others in good faith).

Intellectual Traits Essential to Learning Across the Curriculum

The student acquires the intellectual dispositions that, when developed, direct the right use of the mind.

To meet this requirement, the student will display the following:

- fair-mindedness: (a commitment to treating all viewpoints on their merits alone, without reference to one's own feelings or selfish interests, or the feelings or selfish interests of one's friends, community or nation).

- intellectual autonomy: (a commitment to analyzing and evaluating beliefs on the basis of reason and evidence; thinking for oneself).

- intellectual civility: (a commitment to taking others seriously as thinkers, even if they disagree with us, granting respect to the person and full attention to their views)

- confidence in reason: (a commitment to reasonability, to thinking coherently and logically, to following evidence rather than blind belief).

- intellectual courage: (a willingness to express unpopular beliefs when such beliefs seem more reasonable than popular ones; a willingness to examine one's own beliefs for justifiability).

- intellectual curiosity: (a strong desire to figure things out, to pose and pursue questions of one's own in attempting to make sense of the world).

- intellectual empathy: (a commitment to imaginatively placing oneself in the belief system or point of view of others to appreciate insights available from their perspectives).

- intellectual humility: (a commitment to understanding the nature and extent of one's ignorance, the limitations of one's knowledge) .

- intellectual integrity: (a commitment to be true to one's thinking, to be consistent in the intellectual standards one applies, to practice what one advocates for others, and to honestly admit discrepancies and inconsistencies in one's own thoughts and actions).

- intellectual perseverance: (a commitment to do challenging intellectual work over an extended period of time, despite difficulties, obstacles, and frustrations).

Modes of Thinking Essential to Learning in Every Subject

The student learns to think within the logic of the subjects studied.

To meet this requirement, the student will, using the elements of thought, master essential modes of thinking such as:

- **historical** thinking: posing significant historical questions; analyzing, evaluating, and reconstructing historical interpretations; understanding multiple historical concepts and alternative historical viewpoints; reading historical texts and writing historical essays with insight and understanding; using historical thinking to make intelligent decisions in the present and plans for the future.

- **civic thinking:** posing significant social and civic questions; analyzing, evaluating, and reconstructing interpretations of social trends; understanding multiple social and civic concepts and conflicting social and political viewpoints; reading a wide variety of newspapers and news magazines critically; writing social commentary with insight and understanding; evaluating present social and political practices and policies in the light of social ideals and human rights; using civic and political thinking to make intelligent decisions in the present and plans for the future.

- **scientific thinking:** posing significant scientific questions; analyzing, evaluating, and reconstructing scientific interpretations; formulating plausible scientific concepts, theories and hypotheses, making reasonable scientific predictions, designing scientific experiments, gathering scientific facts, making justifiable scientific inferences; distinguishing scientific from theological reasoning; using scientific thinking to make intelligent decisions in the present and plans for the future.

- **mathematical thinking:** posing significant mathematical questions and problems; analyzing, evaluating, and reconstructing mathematical interpretations and relationships; making justifiable mathematical inferences; mastering mathematical concepts and principles; using mathematical thinking to make intelligent decisions regarding quantitative matters; reading math texts with understanding of the mathematical thinking therein.

- **literary thinking:** posing significant literary questions and problems; analyzing, evaluating, and reconstructing literary interpretations and relationships; making justifiable literary inferences; using literary thinking to make intelligent decisions regarding stories and poems; thinking analytically and critically about literary texts; reading novels, plays, short stories, and poems with insight, understanding and appreciation; reasoning from information in a literary text to plausible interpretations and judgments of appreciation (and being able to explain and defend such interpretations and judgments on reasonable grounds).

Questions You Should Ask of Every Reform Enthusiast

- What is your concept of education?
- What is your concept of an educated person?
- What abilities must persons develop (to be considered educated)?
- What intellectual standards must they acquire?
- What intellectual traits?
- What is your concept of the educational process? (How does one go about educating a person?)
- What intellectual structures are present in all content (that enable students to relate or contrast what they are learning in one subject with what they are learning in other subjects)?
- How should content be presented in the teaching process? (How should history be presented? Science? Math? Literature?)
- How should students learn content? (How should they learn history? Science? Math? Literature?)
- How should we understand the fundamental goal in teaching any given subject?
- When we assess students during the learning process, what should we focus our assessment on?
- How does _____ (insert name of trend or fad) serve a substantive concept of education? Use this question as a lead into questions that probe the relationship of the trend or fad to essential abilities, standards, and traits. Then lead into questions that probe the relationship of the trend or fad to the essential ingredients in the educational process.
- How will it help students analyze and evaluate their own thinking and the thinking of others more effectively?
- How will it help them act reasonably and effectively in their lives?
- How will it help them make self-assessment an integral part of their lives?
- How will it help them master content in diverse disciplines?
- How will it help them become proficient readers, writers, speakers, and listeners?
- How will it help them improve the quality of their lives and the lives of others?
- How will it help them become reasonable and fair-minded persons?
- How will it help them use their reasoning skills to contribute to their own emotional life and that of others?
- How will it help them think, feel, and act effectively and with integrity?

Still Other Questions About the Trend or Fad:

- How will it help us fix the thinking that is running the schools?
- How will it help administrators shift their emphasis from troubleshooting short-range problems, handling complaints, settling disputes, and making sure that legal and bureaucratic requirements are met, to focusing on facilitating the achievement of a substantive education?
- How will it help administrators focus on long-range consequences of the manner in which teachers teach and students learn?
- How will it help make a substantive concept of education an important topic of day-to-day discussion?
- How will it help us overcome the problems of fragmentation and superficial learning?
- How will it help teachers change their focus from day-to-day survival to teaching for substantive learning based on a substantive concept of education?
- How will it help students shift from thinking about the schools either as a place to socialize and have fun or a place to be passively tolerated to thinking about the schools as a place to learn how to learn (for life)?
- How will it help parents develop a substantive concept of education?
- How will it help school board members think in terms of setting long-range goals and broad policies that serve a substantive concept of education?
- How will it help all those who influence or participate in schooling come together as a community of thinkers focused on cultivating an atmosphere and environment conducive to education (substantively conceived)?

Educational Fads and Trends

Now let us turn to our analysis and critique of educational fads and trends. In each case, we provide the essential idea, the proper educational use, and the likely misuse. We have no illusion that our coverage is exhaustive. Rather we exemplify how to get at the root idea of a fad and see its most essential value and danger.

Alignment

Essential Idea: The growing concern with "alignment" in education is connected with a growing recognition that the fragmentation and "incoherence" now existing in school structure, instruction, and learning is unacceptable. Too often what is happening in school does not "add up" to anything substantial, or even intelligible. There are a number of problems contributing to the "non-aligned" (fragmented) state of education today.

One of the contributing factors is the degree to which persons employed in the schools are specialists (narrowly focused on what they do, without effective coordination with others).

Another factor is the failure of mission statements (intended to be a tool of integration and convergence) to say anything clear or substantial. Most mission statements are loose conglomerations of vague, high-sounding, but largely empty phrases pieced together by a committee (in order to present a positive image of the schools to parents and community leaders).

A third factor is found in the design of textbooks. More and more textbooks are virtual encyclopedias, the reading of which one author recently characterized as "a mind-deadening experience."

A fourth factor is the largely unintegrated way teachers themselves originally learned the subjects they now teach. We teach as we were taught. Too frequently teachers passed their college courses largely through rote memorization and cramming before the exam. Their own learning having been fragmented, what they now teach has taken on the character of a list. They teach this and this and that and that, then this and this, then that and that, then this and that, then that and this.

The end result is that little is taught that is substantial or deep. All too often, *quantity covered* substitutes for *quality learned*. To conclude, there is no question but that an emphasis on alignment is important. The question is, what should alignment entail? What precisely are we aligning and how are we aligning it?

Proper Educational Use: *With* a substantive concept of education at the core of schooling, every significant element in the educational process can be set out in integrated fashion: curriculum, teaching methods, textbook use, content coverage, assessment, outcomes, standards, and staff development. Fragmentation and superficiality can be targeted using practical strategies. The intellectual standards, essential abilities, and traits serve as major focuses for what is to be aligned. Curriculum, teaching methods, textbook use, coverage, assessment, outcomes, standards, and staff development should each be examined to determine whether and how they foster these foundations.

Of course, it is not enough to integrate **within** subjects. Integration must be achieved **across** subjects, and that becomes possible only when there is a shared recognition of the one deep common denominator of all subjects, namely that they are all modes of thinking and reasoning and hence all require thinking and reasoning if one is to learn them. In other words, mastering a subject is learning how to reason through a body of content (reasoning about numbers, reasoning about history, reasoning while reading, reasoning while writing, reasoning about plants, animals, social groups, etc.).

Likely Misuse: Without a substantial concept of education as a guide to what needs aligning, alignment is likely to be superficial and misleading. The mere outward appearance of alignment is likely to substitute for genuine and substantial alignment. That mere appearance is easily created by changing verbal descriptions without substantially changing what is being done in the classroom. In other words, expressions may be introduced into the curriculum and mission statement that imply alignment, even though there is no shared substantial concept of education. True alignment is no simple matter since it presupposes an analysis and assessment of all the elements of education viewed through the prism of a substantial conception of education. In the light of it, the teaching of every subject is redesigned. Key organizing ideas for curriculum and instruction are created. Content is rethought as modes of thinking. Assessment is recast to mirror the emphasis on the essential abilities, standards, and traits. Professional development for teachers is focused on the teaching strategies appropriate to a substantial conception of education. All other inservice programs support a substantial conception of education.

Without a substantial concept of education to serve as a guide and test, none of these essential alignments are likely to occur. Instead, the fragmented thinking of educators will remain unexamined while words implying alignment will be scattered throughout curriculum and instructional guides. Teachers will have no conception of how to teach science as scientific thinking or literature as literary thinking. They will not think to teach reading as "the thinking of a skilled reader." Math will not be taught as mathematical thinking.

What is more, thinking itself will not be properly analyzed or assessed. Teachers will lack a concept of the essential structures in thought — and hence will not analyze using those structures.

They will not have been taught how to assess thinking for clarity, accuracy, precision, relevance, depth, breadth, logicalness and significance — and hence they will not do so. Students will fall back on their habits of preparing for tests by memorizing bits and pieces from textbooks or class lectures. The teachers will not know how to teach for such crucial traits as intellectual perseverance or intellectual humility. Without intellectual perseverance students give up as soon as work becomes difficult or challenging. Without intellectual humility students lack an awareness of the extent of their ignorance (and hence are unmotivated to learn).

In short, though alignment is essential to the educational process, what is more important is **what** we are aligning and **how** we are aligning it.

Assessment

Essential Idea: Teaching cannot be effectively designed unless it includes a sound conception of how to assess the nature and quality of student learning. One cannot make adjustments in teaching if one does not know to what extent students are learning what we are intending them to learn. For many years much schooling has been based on false assumptions about student learning. Often we have assumed, for example, that because students had successfully memorized content for a test they actually understood it or could use it effectively when its application to the real world became imperative.

In many ways, the quality of schooling reflects the quality of assessment being used in schooling. For example, if we assess recall and memorization as a major point of emphasis, then we generate masses of citizens skilled only at tasks that require memorization and recall. Or again, if we focus assessment on superficial information that is learned in a fragmented way, we are cultivating minds that are superficial and fragmented.

We must design assessment in light of the primary goals of schooling. This presupposes that we think through these goals and not simply develop goals that are vague, high-sounding, but largely empty of meaning.

It follows that if one of our primary goals is that students become lifelong learners and critical thinkers, then a primary goal in assessment is to determine the extent to which students are learning how to assess and improve their own thinking and learning.

Proper Educational Use: Both educators and students need to learn the fundamental logic of assessment: its contrast with subjective preference, how to set assessment goals, how to ask evaluative questions, how to gather facts relevant to the questions asked, how to set up evaluative criteria, how to fairly apply evaluative criteria to the facts we have gathered. Virtually all human thought and action is permeated with value judgments that require evaluative thought. We must evaluate persons, books, foods, cars, homes, relationships, jobs, schools — everything that can have merit or worth, can help us or harm us.

Therefore, we must include in our design of education a sound conception of how student learning is going to be assessed. We must ensure that there is integration and convergence across the following parameters: the mission statement, the curriculum, the use of textbooks, the design of instruction, and the design of assessment. We must begin with an assessment of that alignment. We must make sure that assessment is focused on a substantive conception of education. The total design of teaching and learning must be so focused.

This means we must assess whether teachers are teaching and students learning the essential abilities, essential standards, and essential traits. We must also assess such matters as how teachers are hired, evaluated, and given professional development training; how administrative policies and practices impact student learning; how student attitudes and work habits impact student learning; how parental support, or lack thereof, impacts student learning.   The total system at work must be evaluated from the perspective of our responsibility to provide all students with a substantive education.

Likely Misuse: It is easy to misunderstand assessment. Assessment should not be seen as good in and of itself. Teachers, students, indeed all of us, continually assess situations, people, experiences. And, unfortunately, we often use inappropriate standards in assessing whatever we are assessing. So there is nothing magic in the *idea* of assessment. What we want to do is to assess *well, reasonably, logically, accurately*.

In the classroom, it is easy to assume that we are effectively monitoring student learning when we are not (again, merely because we are "assessing" it). Typically we miss the most obvious forms of instructional failure. For example, many students are learning to hate math (as a result of math instruction). Many students are learning to dislike school (as a result of instruction in general). Many students are learning that school is a place that does not deal with questions or issues of importance to their world. Many students are learning that when one is learning one should be passive, quiet, take notes, and memorize (when a test is drawing near). None of these "learnings" are intended. And for years we hardly noticed them. Even now we almost never assess the extent to which our instruction is failing in significant ways.

Typically, students are "learning" that knowledge is determined by the teacher. This is connected with the fact that students often get good grades merely by telling teachers what they want to hear--even when students don't understand the meaning of what they are saying. Hence, though many students could define democracy as a government of the people, by the people, and for the people; very few could explain the differences between a government *of*, but not *by* or *for* the people.

What is more, few students have any sense of what it is to be a lifelong learner or what it is to evaluate and assess their thoughts, their emotions, their behavior, their decisions, and their lives. Thus some of the most important ways assessment should be used and fostered are being almost completely ignored in schooling today.

As a result of their instruction, many students confuse assessment with subjective expressions of likes and dislikes. Many students, and far too many teachers, think that all evaluation is arbitrary and nothing more than a mere personal opinion. They fail to see that all genuine assessment culminates in a reasoned judgment, can therefore be questioned in a number of ways, and requires proper application of intellectual standards.

We have a long way to go before we begin to expect quality assessment of significant learning, primarily because teachers themselves do not, as a rule, have a clear concept of significant learning. We have a long way to go before we begin to teach students the nature of assessment and how to make disciplined self-assessment an integral part of their lives.

Authentic Pedagogy & Assessment

Essential Idea: The push for "authentic pedagogy" is based on the insight that students will not be appropriately prepared if they are not given tasks and tests that reflect the actual problems they will eventually face in their work and personal life. It follows that students should be taught content so that they truly understand it and, most especially, grasp how to apply it in the world. If they learn in this way, their learning will be "authentic." Authentic pedagogy and assessment often refer not only to skills and abilities relevant to functioning in the real world, but more specifically, to effectively dealing with complex problems and issues, similar to those we all face as humans living a complex human life.

Examples of authentic assessments often include:

- performance of the skills, or demonstrating use of a particular knowledge.
- simulations and roleplays.
- studio portfolios, strategically selecting items.
- exhibitions and displays.

The idea is that classroom experiences should reflect real life as much as possible, and authentic assessments should evaluate the extent to which students will be able to use their skills in real world situations.

Proper Educational Use: There is an excellent match between the drive for "authentic" pedagogy and assessment and the need to focus instruction on a substantive concept of education, for what makes a substantive concept of education powerful is that it embodies the learning most essential to success in everyday life. There is nothing more useful in the world than thinking that is clear, accurate, precise, relevant, deep, logical, and significant. To think and behave successfully in the world, one needs to monitor one's thinking for main purposes and goals and think in a disciplined way to achieve those purposes and goals. One needs to formulate accurately the most important questions, problems, and issues and gather key relevant data and information that will solve the problems one faces. A similar point may be made for each essential ability and each essential trait. For example, if one lacks confidence in reason, one will not bother to gather and respect evidence. One will egocentrically ignore sound reasoning when one wants to.

So, certainly we should regularly review what we are teaching to determine the extent to which what we are teaching is a good match with what we want students eventually to be able to understand and to do in the world. When there is a poor match, we should modify our teaching accordingly. For example, if we are having students memorize formulas in math class, we need to ask ourselves if memorizing formulas is what enables people to do math in the real world. Or again, if studying history involves memorizing historical facts to repeat on tests that assess such memorizing, then we need to question why we are teaching history in the first place. We must ask ourselves whether we believe that historical thinking is an important part of success in life, and if so, how it can be fostered in the classroom.

It is important to design instruction so that it lays a solid foundation for success in life. Students must be taught with a clear sense of what kinds of challenges and problems they will later face. Their tasks in the classroom should mirror those later challenges and problems. If they will later have to deal with complexity, then we should design instruction so that they must deal with complexity today in the classroom. If later they will have to define and explain problems and consider alternative strategies for solving them, then we must assign tasks in school that require students to define and explain problems and consider and evaluate alternative strategies for their solution. If students are later going to have to evaluate their own thinking and assess their own work, then we must teach them today to understand what evaluation and assessment require and assign them tasks which require them to evaluate their own thinking and work.

As school is presently structured, students rarely engage in disciplined evaluative reasoning. Nevertheless, evaluative reasoning is essential to both learning and practice of every academic subject. If students do not learn how to assess their own work, conduct, emotional responses, thoughts, and judgments, they will not be prepared for any important dimension of life. As parents, workers, consumers, and citizens we are continually called upon to assess. If we do not know how to do it, if we confuse it with our subjective reactions and preferences, our quality of life suffers.

In short, we should teach students to regularly assess their own work using appropriate intellectual standards because the proper application of these standards is necessary to living a rational life. We should teach students to regularly analyze reasoning because reasoning is ever present in human life and the quality of one's life depends on the quality of one's reasoning. We should teach students to develop intellectual virtues, traits and dispositions because these are necessary to fair-minded critical thought.

Likely Misuse: It is easy to misunderstand instruction and assessment. Instructional tasks which appear to foster genuine understanding may not in fact mirror what students will experience in their lives. To mirror reality, classroom structures and "authentic" assessments must focus on the *improvement of reasoning* so that students will, as they live their lives, reason better having been through these programs.

In considering the common tenets of authentic assessment —

- performance of the skills, or demonstrating use of a particular knowledge
- simulations and role plays
- studio portfolios, strategically selecting items
- exhibitions and displays

We might ask the following questions:

- What skills are being fostered and how will these skills enable students to reason better in the complex world they will face?
- How do we determine the "particular knowledge" students will need, given that adults change careers seven times in a lifetime, on average? And then how can students demonstrate that they would use this knowledge in real world situations?
- What types of simulations and roleplays will be used, and how will they mirror reality? How can we ensure that students use intellectual standards in assessing their own and others' reasoning in simulations and roleplays, and that application of standards will transfer to real-life reasoning situations?
- What will be contained in these portfolios and what specific reasoning abilities, skills, and traits will they foster?
- What types of exhibitions and displays will be used and how will their use aid students in reasoning better through real-life complex problems?

In other words, looking at typical "authentic" assessments, it's not clear that they would foster deep learning or develop understandings critical to the educated mind. It will depend upon what each assessment specifically entails and how it is used in teaching and learning.

Put another way, those who advocate for authentic learning often describe authentic learning in ways that require significant contextualization. It is easy to talk about being rigorous and requiring serious intellectual work, but what such rigor and serious work consists in needs to be explicated within a well-specified, substantive concept of education.

For example, regarding "authentic assessment," most students and many teachers have little understanding of the difference between objective **evaluation** and subjective **reaction**. The result is that the standards used in assessment are typically either very task specific (and hence not very generalizable) or arbitrary (reflecting highly subjective preferences). When students are called on to evaluate work, they often do little more than state what they like or dislike. Authentic instruction and assessment should be linked with a vision of assessment that clearly distinguishes genuine evaluation from mere subjective reaction. Both students and teachers need to grasp the fact that all genuine assessment culminates in a reasoned judgment and hence can be questioned (and cross-checked) in a number of distinctive ways. For instance, we can question the purpose, the formulation of the question, the information collected, the criteria or standards used, and the way the standards were applied.

According to Fred Newmann and Gary Wehlage pedagogy is "authentic" only if it:

1. is "linked to a vision for high quality student learning," and

2. leads to "teaching that promotes high quality standards," that is, teaching that "requires students to think, to develop in-depth understanding, and to apply academic learning to important, realistic problems." (Successful School Restructuring, Center on Organization and Restructuring of Schools, p 3.)

Block Scheduling

Essential Idea: The idea behind "block scheduling" is usually tied to the general idea of restructuring schools. It represents one of the advocated changes in "structure"— in this case, a change in how time is divided into instructional periods. The thinking behind the idea is something like this: In the traditional school, the school day is divided into so many periods that too much time is involved in moving about and in getting settled. As a result, there is too little time in the traditional class for getting into a topic in depth. The proposed solution is fewer subjects and more time "blocked" out in longer periods that lend themselves to in-depth work.

Proper Educational Use: There can be no question but that the traditional middle school and high school are often structured into so many instructional periods per day that there is very little time in any given period to learn anything in-depth. The idea of teaching fewer subjects in longer time blocks in greater depth is an excellent idea, in general. The more time we have with students, the deeper we can generally go within a topic, issue, subject.

Likely Misuse: The main pitfall in block scheduling is that no problems are automatically solved by having more time dedicated to a subject on any given day. The key is not time but what teachers do with it. If teachers use it for longer lectures or for more busywork, nothing will really change. The goal, then, is to use the longer time blocks *effectively*. To achieve this goal requires long-term staff development in which teachers begin to shift their habits of instruction as they shift their conception of instruction (including how to focus on key organizing ideas, how to require reasoning rather than subjective reactions, how to teach for depth of understanding and student self-assessment).

Once again, the key is whether the longer blocks provide a way of focusing on the abilities, standards, and traits of mind essential to a substantive conception of education, and in helping students learn how to use those abilities, traits and standards in thinking within the logic of the subjects they are studying. This requires, of course, that the teachers learn how to model thinking for the students (e.g., historical, mathematical, scientific thinking), how to engage the students in that thinking (by specific classroom activities and assignments), and how to hold the students responsible for evaluating their thinking (as they think and after they think). By itself block scheduling solves none of our problems.

Bloom's Taxonomy

Essential Idea: The idea behind Bloom's Taxonomy is the notion that teaching lends itself typically to a predictable order in teaching and learning.

- **Knowledge.** First, there must be something to learn, some identifiable "knowledge" to acquire.

- **Comprehension.** Second, to gain that knowledge one must initially "comprehend" it in some way.

- **Application.** Third, comprehension is abstract and not "concrete" until one can "apply" the concept to cases, situations in the real world.

- **Analysis.** Fourth, to more deeply understand an idea one must be able to break it down into components.

- **Synthesis.** Fifth, to understand an idea one has "analyzed" requires that one can connect the parts into a whole and see their interrelationships.

- **Evaluation.** Sixth, to grasp what one has learned one must "evaluate" that learning for its completeness and accuracy.

Proper Educational Use: If one qualifies the basic "steps" delineated above and limits the claims made by each to modest ones, then the taxonomy has some usefulness. For example, it is impossible to give students knowledge to start the learning process. Teachers can, however, have in mind something they want students to learn and can present that content in some way to students for processing. This processing and initial "comprehension" will be closely interrelated. Once students have some initial comprehension, teachers can help them ground that comprehension in examples (application to the real world).

Here is one way to put the first three stages of Bloom's Taxonomy.

1. Have the students state in their own words what they are trying to learn (initial knowledge).
2. Have the students elaborate in their own words what they understand in their initial statement (initial comprehension).
3. Have the students exemplify in their own words what they have stated and elaborated, using their own examples from their life experience (initial application).

This three-step process, which is a beginning place for all learning (demonstrating the ability to state, elaborate, and exemplify the meaning of a concept, idea, etc.) is an example of the proper use of the stages that Bloom calls Knowledge, Comprehension, and Application.

The second three steps (Analysis, Synthesis, and Evaluation) can be similarly explained. Initial comprehension and exemplification can be followed by the process of breaking down knowledge into eight component parts:

- the *purpose* of the knowledge,
- the *question* that drives one to seek the knowledge,
- the *information* that underlies the knowledge,
- the *concepts* that organize the knowledge,
- the *assumptions* embedded in the knowledge,
- the *conclusions* we come to in arriving at the knowledge,
- the *implications* of the knowledge, and

- the *point of view* that enables us to put all the parts together in an integrated vision.

Once we can break down knowledge into components (analysis), we can then seek to put the parts together into a systematic, integrated whole (synthesis). And finally, we can evaluate our thinking to determine whether it is clear, accurate, precise, relevant, deep, broad, logical, significant and justifiable (all of which must be applied, of course, as relevant to the issue or problem being analyzed).

Likely Misuse: To effectively apply Bloom's categories to instruction, teachers must think through each category each time they are used. Otherwise, these categories are likely to be used superficially.

- First, teachers should focus learning on significant knowledge (helping students thereby ground themselves in fundamental and important ideas). In other words, knowledge in and of itself is neither good nor bad. Teachers need to think through ideas, distinguishing the deep from the superficial, the important from the unimportant, and focus on those that matter most in learning.

- Second, the order of the *steps* can be varied in accordance with the demands of context and situation. In other words, the steps should not necessarily be seen as steps, but rather important concepts or processes in learning. For example, there is a form of evaluation appropriate to each of Bloom's *steps* in learning. Evaluation cannot be restricted to the final step in learning. Or to take another example, when we say knowledge, we might mean initial understanding, or we might mean deep ownership of an idea. Deep ownership or knowledge of an idea may take many months or even years to comprehend.

- Third, each of the steps in analysis can itself involve stating, elaborating, and exemplifying (thus analysis itself can involve several intellectual processes and require multiple abilities).

- Finally, Bloom's taxonomy does not define critical thinking. Rather critical thinking enables teachers to use Bloom's taxonomy effectively, should they choose to use it.

In short, teachers can think critically or uncritically while using the categories of the taxonomy.

Brain-Based Teaching & Learning

Essential Idea: Since the human brain unquestionably provides the main physiological and neurological basis for human learning, it is reasonable to think that information about the nature of the brain might provide us with information about the nature of human learning and hence about how to enhance learning through instruction. The idea behind brain-based teaching and learning, then, is to study the results of the most current research into brain functions in order to figure out how to design instruction that is compatible with those findings.

Proper Educational Use: Research into the brain can at best provide us with *hypotheses* about pedagogy and learning. These hypotheses are by-products of someone's interpretation of the significance of some research on brain functions. In any case, these hypotheses must be tested against what we know about the human "mind" from common experience. For example, we know that human minds sometimes function self-deceptively, that humans often "protect" themselves from potential guilt feelings by construing the facts in a self-serving and misleading manner. Humans typically see things in ways that justify pursuing their vested interest. They find ways to make that pursuit look like a moral crusade.

These are "facts" about (a significant slice of) human behavior. Brain research, therefore, cannot prove that self-deception does not occur, for we know through experience that it does. What brain research can do is to help illuminate how the brain functions when we engage in self-deception. As things now stand, however, brain research sheds little light on how the brain deceives itself. Our present knowledge of self-deception comes from direct experience and from studies that focus on self-deception from a non-neurological stand-point.

We can now generalize from this example (of brain research and human self-deception) to brain research in general and what we know about the mind in general. We have been gathering facts about the human mind for literally thousands of years.

It is easy to state any number of important truths about the human mind that are not subject to "disproof" through brain research. Consider the following:

1. Beliefs about the family, personal relationships, marriage, childhood, obedience, religion, politics, schooling, etc. are significantly (though not exclusively) shaped by cultural, national, and familial influences.
2. As humans we have a strong tendency to think egocentrically and sociocentrically about the world.
3. We tend to assume that others are correct when they agree with us and incorrect when they do not.
4. We tend to assume that the groups to which we belong — our religion, our country, our friends — are special, and better than the groups to which others belong.
5. We tend to assume that what coincides with what we want to believe is true.
6. We tend to assume that what advances our wealth, power, or position is justified.

There are many such facts about the human mind that brain research at some time in the future may help us explain neurologically. It would be a mistake, however, to think that we are close to those explanations or that the explanations in themselves will help us determine how to "minimize" our pathological mental tendencies.

What we need to do when exploring current interpretations of present brain research, then, is 1) be cautious about inferences made about teaching and learning (they are *interpretations* of research data, not necessarily facts in themselves), 2) qualify any interpretations by what we already know about the mind independent of brain research, and 3) remember that the key question is, "How does this interpretation of brain functioning further our ability to foster intellectual abilities?"

Pitfalls: There are a number of dangers potentially inherent in translating "results" from brain research into "designs" for teaching or "strategies" for learning. One of the most important is based in the fact that the "results" from brain research come in two forms: "hard" data and "soft" interpretations. On the one hand, the hard data from research comes closest to being "scientifically" trustworthy; however, it provides us with little help in designing teaching and learning precisely because it has no clear-cut implications for us to follow in that design (without some accompanying, mediating, "interpretation"). On the other hand, interpretations based in brain research are often controversial precisely because they are "soft." They are not science, but relatively rough attempts to take the science of the day and translate it in order to put it to some use (usually in an area for which its initial development was not intended).

The history of education is filled with attempts of educators to translate from the science of the day to "truths" of pedagogy. This history alone should make us very cautious. Consider the energy and enthusiasm that accompanied the attempt to translate behavioral science (over the last 40 years) into educational reality. Now brain research enthusiasts are playing down the research of behavioral science and applauding the research of neuronal, biochemical science. The fact is that anyone attempting to move back and forth between "science" and "pedagogy" had better be an excellent critical thinker in both domains. What is more, such a person should be familiar with the history of such attempts and the common results of them (a distorting of the teaching process in one direction, only to be counter-distorted in another direction by the next new wave of "popularized" research).

A second danger comes from the very justification often used in brain-based teaching and learning, namely, that research into the nature and operations of the brain is a massive field in a state of accelerating change. Not too long ago, many popularizers were mesmerized by the prominence of the "right" and "left" brain theory. We were told with great solemnity that everyone was either a "right-brained" or a "left-brained" person, that our various thoughts were produced by either the right or left brain, that we should therefore identify which brain was prominent in our various students and teach accordingly. Present brain-based enthusiasts have abandoned these sweeping hemispheric pronouncements. (while presenting us with new "authoritative truths"). It is clear that it makes little sense to radically shift our pedagogy every few years to "fit" the latest popularized notions from research.

Character Education

Essential Idea: The idea behind character education is a concern with "unethical" behavior in our society. Those who advocate this approach argue that we have a responsibility to foster ethics in our young people so they will contribute to our collective well being rather than become habituated to anti-social, self-serving behavior. They argue for the need to develop citizens who have internalized fundamental ethical values and principles and, as a result, live lives that embody those values and principles. Character education is successful, then, to the extent that it helps cultivate citizens who are kind, thoughtful, considerate, empathic, honest, responsible, and just. No reasonable person would argue against this goal.

Proper Educational Use: Character education succeeds only to the extent that those who design it can clearly distinguish two very different processes:

1. the indoctrination of students into socially approved beliefs and behaviors, on the one hand, and
2. the cultivating of universal ethical principles and traits, on the other.

The danger is that administrators and teachers are not experts in "ethical principles and values."

Like most humans they have a tendency to make judgments about right and wrong that are a confused product of ethical values, social taboos, religious teachings and legal facts. Put another way, many teachers have not been taught the essential difference between social values (which vary from society to society) and ethical principles (which are invariable from society to society, and apply to all sentient creatures). Consequently, when they set out to teach students ethical principles, teachers often inadvertently teach for social conformity. Genuine ethical development is then confused with social and ideological conformity.

So, though nearly everyone gives at least lip service to a universal common core of general ethical principles — for example, that it is morally wrong to cheat, deceive, exploit, abuse, harm, or steal from others, that everyone has a moral responsibility to respect the rights of others, including their freedom and well-being, to help those most in need of help, to seek the common good and not merely their own self-interest and egocentric pleasures, to strive to make this world more just and humane — few have developed the ability to distinguish ethical judgments from social, political, religious, and legal ones.

Students, then, need practice in discriminating between ethical principles and social rules. They need practice in ethical reasoning, not indoctrination into the view that one nation rather than another determines these ethical principles. Students certainly need opportunities to learn basic ethical principles, but more importantly they need opportunities to apply them to real and imagined cases, and to develop insight into both genuine and pseudo ethics. They especially need to come to terms with the pitfalls of human moralizing, to recognize the ease with which we mask self-interest or egocentric desires with high-sounding ethical language.

In a substantive approach to ethics, students learn the art of self-critique, of ethical self-examination, to become attuned to the pervasive everyday pitfalls of moral judgment: intolerance, self-deception, and uncritical conformity. They learn to recognize the misuse of ethical language at the service of social and political ideologies, emotionalism, and/or vested interests. They learn to distinguish clear-cut cases of ethical right and wrong from controversial cases (requiring the examination of argumentation from multiple points of view). They learn to identify social witch-hunts that prosper in the guise of ethical crusades. They become familiar with documents that articulate universal ethical principles, like the Declaration of Independence and the UN Declaration of Human Rights. They develop ethical humility, ethical courage, ethical integrity, ethical perseverance, empathy and fairmindedness. These traits are compatible with the holding of many belief systems (whether conservative, liberal, theistic, atheistic, etc.).

In a substantively designed curriculum, consideration of ethical issues is integrated into diverse subject areas, including literature, science, history, civics, and society. This requires that teachers understand the abilities, standards, and traits of an educated person and that they understand how to foster those abilities using the modes of thinking that define the curriculum. For most of them, this requires professional staff development in critical thinking applied to ethical reasoning. For example, at present most teachers do not have a clear understanding of the differences between ethical *principles* (which tell us in a general way what we ought and ought not to do), *perspectives* (which characterize the world in ways which lead to an organized way of interpreting it — conservatism, liberalism, theism, etc.) and *facts* (which can be distorted to fit a particular point of view).

Likely Misuse: The problem, then, is not at the level of general principles. Very few people in the world take themselves to oppose human rights or stand for injustice, slavery, exploitation, deception, dishonesty, theft, greed, starvation, ignorance, falsehood, and human suffering. On the other hand, no nation or group has special ownership over any general ethical principle. Indeed, virtually all social groups tend to uncritically assume that their social rules and taboos are an embodiment of universal ethics. Lacking these fundamental distinctions, teachers are likely to encourage either absolutistic thinking or ethical and intellectual relativism, both of which result in dangerous forms of pseudo-ethics in the world (for example, social witch hunts, persecution, intolerance, invasion of privacy, misuse of the criminal justice system, and narrow-mindedness). The misuse then is a predictable "use" for all of those who have not learned how to distinguish the ethical from the religious, the social, the legal, and the ideological. This is the vast majority of teachers, administrators, and citizens.[2]

Charter Schools

Essential Idea: The idea behind the charter school movement is that the public school system is not able to reform itself because it is hamstrung by legal and bureaucratic constraints and a rigid tradition and that only a school freed from the constraints of school district bureaucracy will be able to create needed changes. And unlike private schools, which naturally enjoy this freedom, charter schools are open-access and free to the public. Charter schools are schools which are "chartered," each with their own academic emphasis and special approach to change and excellence. It is assumed that when parents are able to choose between charter schools and traditional public schools, the competition engendered will serve as an incentive to improve the quality of public school performance.

Proper Educational Use: It is plausible that increased autonomy produced through increased freedom from bureaucratic constraints is likely to produce some change in classroom instruction. However, it in no way guarantees long-term, substantive change. Change may be change for the worse, or merely cosmetic in nature. For charter schools to be genuinely successful, they must be guided by insightful leadership. The principal and at least some of the teachers must be well-informed enough to seek long-term objectives, avoid superficial or empty rhetoric (such as is found in most mission statements), recognize that the quality of instruction is dependent on the quality of thinking that designs and implements instruction, grasp that the quality of learning is dependent on the quality of the thinking that produces that learning, and understand that only a foundational commitment to intellectual standards and critical thinking across the curriculum will produce the kind of change that substantively improves how students learn and grow.

---

2   For a more in-depth understanding of ethics, see Paul, R. and Elder, L. (2006). *Understanding the Foundations of Ethical Reasoning*. Dillon Beach, CA: Foundation for Critical Thinking, www.criticalthinking.org

Pitfalls: Charter schools succeed, like those which shift to school-based management, only to the extent that teachers and administrators have a sound understanding of what impedes high quality learning and what needs to be done to cultivate it, and are willing to make a long-term commitment to facilitate it. However, research conducted by the Center for Critical Thinking, (Paul, et al., California Teacher Preparation, 1997), in combination with extensive experience in assessing teachers' performance at professional development workshops, strongly implies that very few teachers presently have the skills essential for the paradigm shift in instruction required for substantive change. For example, research demonstrates that few teachers today understand what critical thinking is or how to teach for it. What is more, this understanding cannot be developed in the short run.

To spell this out further, very few teachers understand intellectual standards or can distinguish them from what are commonly called "rubrics." Few teachers are comfortable with either theoretical questions or abstractions (both of which are essential to understanding of, and teaching for, disciplined thinking). Very few teachers know how to teach math as mathematical thinking, science as scientific thinking, geography as geographical thinking. Very few teachers know how to integrate ideas within their subject, or across subjects, or how to foster effective problem solving or communication. The result is that even with the freedom of a charter school, teachers and their administrators are likely to design systems and instruction in ways that produce superficial rather than substantive change.

Choice (Vouchers & Privatization)

Essential Idea: The essential idea behind "choice-based" strategies for the improvement of education is the same idea that stands behind capitalism as an economic system. The notion is that if schools were forced to compete for students (as businesses are forced to compete for customers), then schools would be forced to improve the quality of their instruction (or fail for want of students). At present, there is little incentive for schools to improve since they will continue to receive public funds whether they improve or not.

There are many variations and alternative strategies for putting this basic idea into practice. One is that private schools should be allowed to compete with public schools. Another is that public schools should be forced to compete with each other (but not with private schools). One common vehicle for this competition is a "voucher" (a certificate representing a fixed amount of money redeemable by schools chosen by parents for each child). When the competition involves for-profit private schools as well as public schools, then the concept of "privatization" is also involved. Privatization can also be introduced by taking "bids" on the running of whole school systems.

As with the concept of charter schools, the basic thinking is that the twin vehicles of "choice" and "competition" will force improvement. As long as public schools exist as a monopoly with guaranteed numbers of students, why should they improve? Why not let private investors enter into the school "design" competition? Since "for-profit" economics has worked in industry, why not "for-profit" education? What is more, if we are going to save money by outsourcing a wide variety of school services, why not outsource instruction itself?

Proper Educational Use: It is premature to judge the effectiveness of this strategy since few experiments have been conducted under this model. It is likely that the effectiveness will vary in accordance with particular design. Some designs might work while others fail. It seems inappropriate and unreasonable to simply rule out the possibility that it might bring about improvement in instruction.

Pitfalls: There are dangers inherent in the use of the model of competition between schools. The most significant is that of ensuring a level playing field. For example, if public schools are forced to compete with private ones and private schools refuse to admit the more "costly" special education students, then the competition is not really fair. A second important difficulty is in determining appropriate assessment measures to use in assessing the quality of the product "delivered." The "choice" model assumes that parents themselves are good judges (or at least as good as that of traditional educators) of the quality of education. This may or may not be true. Some parents may be satisfied with schooling that indoctrinates their children into a narrow political or religious ideology.

In any case, vouchers and privatization cannot be expected to guarantee a substantive education for a greater number of children unless there is evidence that parents will tend to opt for schools that foster deep learning. Unless and until parents have a substantive concept of education clearly in mind, this is unlikely.

Constructivism

Essential Idea: The essential idea behind a constructivist orientation is the notion that students learn only that knowledge that they actively "construct" in their own minds. I cannot learn for you and you cannot learn for me. The teacher cannot inject knowledge into the heads of students. The student cannot gain knowledge through passive listening or mindless repetition. Rather, the job of teaching is that of designing instruction so that students construct deep and abiding understandings through active intellectual work. For students to construct a new idea, they must read the idea, write the idea, speak the idea, and think the idea into their system (of ideas). Constructivism emphasizes the limitations of traditional didactic teaching, which they see as sacrificing depth of understanding for superficial content coverage. The problem of instruction becomes, from the constructivist standpoint, the problem of creating activities which result in students working a new idea into a system of ideas in their heads. The envisioned result is not perfect understanding (since any new idea is influenced by the ideas students already have, many of them flawed), but better understanding.

Educational Use: The idea of constructivism is traceable to thinkers like Piaget who emphasized that "human knowledge is essentially active." For Piaget, "to know is to assimilate reality into systems." It is to construct networks of thoughts and actions which are integrated by the work of the mind. Hence, to understand the learning of children, Piaget often asked them open-ended questions that enabled them to explain what they were learning in terms that made sense to them. What he found out, of course, is that children are often learning something quite different from what we think they are learning. The systems of meanings by which they interpret school content reflect the immaturity of their minds. We need frequently to remind ourselves to discover what students really think (beneath the surface of what they say). We need to find out what meanings they are inwardly, and often privately, constructing as they engage in learning inside and outside of school.

Unfortunately much of today's instruction and testing do not determine student systems of meaning and it is often possible for students to get good grades by relying on rote memorization and cramming. They then select the correct "true" or "false" options often without fully understanding what is meant by any of the options. They may even be able to mouth correct definition without at all understanding the meaning of the concept they are focused on or its important implications.

Constructivists realize that lower level student learning strategies do not result in personal construction. They are aware of the problem of short-term memorization. They realize that when we emphasize a constructivist approach to learning, we force students to process what they are learning in a deeper way. Students must then interweave what they are learning (at any given time) with other things previously learned.

Likely Misuse: Having recognized that active learning is a necessary condition to higher order learning, we must not assume that it is a sufficient condition. Thus the active "construction" of meaning in and of itself is not sufficient. Let us not forget that the construction of ideas is used in the learning of criminal behavior, in standard peer group learning, and in the socialization processes that result in prejudice, shared illusions, and stereotypes. Gossip, hatred, fear and even math anxiety are all "constructed" in the minds of students all over the world every day. The group influence that occurs in gangs provides a powerful example of undesirable construction of ideas whereby gang members together create meanings that enable them to behave in manipulative, hurtful, and even deadly ways.

If construction in learning is to go beyond uncritical construction, it must embody clear-cut self-assessing processes whereby students raise their learning to a more self-critical level. Students must learn, in other words, to probe their own thinking: seeking and eliminating mistakes that impede excellence in thought. Students must develop the ability and propensity to assess their learning as they are learning, to assess the ideas they are constructing in their minds as they are learning those ideas. They must learn and regularly use appropriate standards for doing so — standards such as clarity, accuracy, precision, depth, breadth, fairmindedness and logicalness.

Students must learn to routinely ask such questions as "Are we thinking clearly enough?" "Are we sure that what we are saying is accurate?" "Do we need to be more precise?" "Are we sticking to the question at issue?" "Are we dealing with the complexities in the question?" "Do we need to consider another perspective or point of view?" "Are our assumptions justifiable or are they faulty?" "Is our purpose fair, or are we only concerned about advancing our own desires?" "Does our argument seem logical, or is it disjointed, lacking cohesion?"

Such questions must become part of the routine process students use in the privacy of their own thinking when constructing ideas in their minds.

Furthermore, intellectual standards must be applied to all of the important structures in thought: to its guiding goal or purpose, to the central question, to the information used in reasoning through the question, to the judgments made in considering the information, to the concepts guiding the judgments, to the assumptions that underlie the judgments, and to the implications that follow from it.

Students must learn to use information and language accurately and precisely to ensure that the information they use is relevant to the issue at hand. Students must come to understand that when they are addressing a complex issue, they must explicitly deal with its complexities and consider differing relevant points of view.

In short, the active construction of meaning is not enough. That construction must be disciplined throughout by careful application of the intellectual standards that keep the best thinking on track. Thinking does not naturally actively engage appropriate standards. In fact, most students (and people in general, for that matter) are naturally drawn to use (because they have actively constructed) standards for assessing thinking which are both egocentric and sociocentric. Most people agree with only that which agrees with what they already believe (egocentric) and that which agrees with what those around them believe (sociocentric).

These natural unintellectual constructions are not easily overcome. Rather they are effectively dealt with only when appropriate intellectual standards are carefully cultivated over a considerable period of time. They are effectively dealt with only through increasing commitment on the part of students to developing their minds as educated persons.

Cooperative Learning

Essential Idea: The idea behind cooperative learning is the notion that students can learn more when they work together, for working together results in the pooling of knowledge and helping each other learn more than they would alone. It is also argued that the world of business increasingly needs people who are good team players and that cooperative learning in the schools prepares students for a team playing role at work.

Proper Educational Use: The basic idea behind cooperative learning is a good one. First, if instruction is appropriately designed, students of high ability can help improve the thinking of less skilled students through cooperative learning. Any structure that requires students to give voice to what they are learning (to write it, speak it, explain and exemplify it to others) fosters learning, both in the person giving voice and the person responding with questions (questions that, for example, encourage the first student to explain more).

Furthermore, when students learn to give one another high quality feedback on their intellectual work, the work of students both giving the feedback and receiving feedback is improved. Put another way, when students help other students identify deficiencies in their thinking, they learn to better identify deficiencies in their own thinking. *It is in teaching that we learn.*

The second argument for cooperative learning is also a good one. Learning to work effectively with others is clearly desirable and useful. It is an important life skill often missing in schooling. This includes learning to enter other points of view in a fair-minded way, to reason empathically within conflicting viewpoints.

In the classroom, various cooperative learning strategies could be employed, including having students work in pairs teaching each other key concepts, putting students into groups of three or four and giving them problems to work through, etc.

Yet the essential component of any cooperative learning assignment or process is its use of intellectual standards. By intellectual standards we mean standards that can be applied to reasoning (independent of domain), standards such as clarity, precision, logicalness, accuracy, relevance, breadth, depth and fairness. When we help students internalize these standards whether working alone or with others, students develop intellectual skills essential to the educated mind.

Likely Misuse: It is important to recognize, however, that cooperative learning does not in and of itself necessarily imply high caliber thinking. Indeed students can "cooperatively learn" either in a high quality or low quality way. We do not want students to engage in group work without consideration of the implications thereof. After all, gang members routinely engage in a form of cooperative learning, as do fascist regimes. Rather we want students to work in groups in an *intellectually responsible* manner. They can do so only if they understand and use appropriate intellectual standards. For example, without intellectual standards, student groups can easily misunderstand the nature of their work. They can think through complex problems in a superficial way — each superficial thinker reinforcing the superficial thinking of the others. "Yeah, that sounds good. I like that answer!" Without intellectual standards, groups can easily fail to consider the logical implications of their reasoning. Without intellectual standards, groups can easily fail to clarify the question embodied by the issue. Without intellectual standards, groups can easily pursue purposes that are not justifiable. Without intellectual standards, groups can easily fail to consider information relevant to their problem. Without intellectual standards, groups can easily fail to check information for accuracy before using it in their reasoning. Without intellectual standards, groups can easily use concepts in intellectually sloppy ways.

In short, cooperative learning in and of itself will not develop the reasoning abilities of students. Cooperative mislearning is a danger throughout. Only when cooperative learning is used in an intellectually disciplined way is its power realized in a fully productive manner.

Core Knowledge

Essential Idea: The "Core Knowledge" movement[3] was established by E. D. Hirsch, Jr., author of *Cultural Literacy: What Every American Needs to Know* and *The Schools We Need and Why We Don't Have Them*. It is an "educational reform" movement based on the premise that a grade-by-grade core of common learning is necessary to ensure a sound and fair elementary education. According to the Core Knowledge Foundation, Hirsch has argued that "for the sake of academic excellence, greater fairness, and higher literacy, early schooling should provide a solid, specific, shared core curriculum in order to help children establish strong foundations of knowledge." The content of this core curriculum has been outlined in two

---

3   The quotes in this section were taken from the Core Knowledge Foundation website: www.coreknowledgefoundation.org, March 2007.

books and states explicitly "what students should learn at each grade level… the Core Knowledge Sequence represents the common ground upon which a faculty meets and collaborates to teach a sequenced, coherent curriculum. In this cumulative curriculum, the knowledge and skills learned each year become the students' foundation for learning in subsequent years."

According to *Core Knowledge*, "Children learn new knowledge by building upon what they already know. It's important to begin building foundations of knowledge in the early grades because that's when children are most receptive, and because academic deficiencies in the first six grades can permanently impair the quality of later schooling. The most powerful tool for later learning is not an abstract set of procedures (such as "problem solving") but a broad base of knowledge in many fields."

"Literacy depends on shared knowledge. To be literate means, in part, to be familiar with a broad range of knowledge taken for granted by speakers and writers. For example, when sportscasters refer to an upset victory as 'David knocking off Goliath,' or when reporters refer to a 'threatened presidential veto,' they are assuming that their audience shares certain knowledge."

The idea behind the "core knowledge" movement, then, is that there is a definable "core" of information that everyone must know in order to function well within in their culture.

Proper Educational Use: It is possible to modify the Hirschian notion of "core" knowledge to one that is more compatible with *fostering the educated mind* through the development of intellectual skills. In that case, we focus on the core ideas and concepts, principles and theories, which are at the root of various domains of thought. In teaching, biology, for example, we would then focus on the core concepts and principles of biology, but teach them as embedded in a domain of thought: biological thinking. In principle, then, there is good reason to focus on *core* ideas and principles, but this is a far cry from what has been advocated by those who have published definitive lists, concepts and information erroneously defined as "core."

Likely Misuse: It is very easy for a focus on a body of information to become an occasion for rote memorization which typically leads to short term recall and superficial understanding. When there is no deeper organizing idea than that of *content to be covered in a specific sequence*, and lacking the necessary organizer of *thinking* that content into one's thinking in a disciplined and permanent way at the heart of the process, it is unlikely deep learning will occur.

The Core Knowledge Foundation implies that students can somehow learn information without thinking it through in a meaningful way. The idea seems to be something like this: *Give students lots of information and "knowledge" and then they will have that knowledge when they need it.* But how are students to gain knowledge without thinking that knowledge into their thinking? Moreover, without focusing explicitly on skills and traits of mind, how will teachers know that students are thinking content into their thinking in *a responsible way*?

The very fact that "Core Knowledge" asserts "The most powerful tool for later learning is not an abstract set of procedures (such as "problem solving") but a broad base of knowledge in many fields," is itself evidence that the importance of thinking in learning is misunderstood in this philosophy, and takes a back seat to taking in lots of information in a set sequence. To learn anything well, to work it into their thinking, students must use abstractions every day in the classroom, and they must use, in a sense, abstract procedures or processes for doing so. First, every idea within every subject is an abstraction because every idea within every subject is conceptual. And second, conceptual procedures are used whenever students, or indeed anyone, thinks ideas into their thinking. For example, to learn an idea, the student must be able to state, elaborate and exemplify it in their thinking. They must be able to demonstrate that they can and will apply that idea when the idea is relevant. All of this requires abstract processes. Otherwise, merely rote and not true "understanding" occurs.

Moreover, how are we to know that teachers themselves are thinking critically about the content they are expected to cover? How are we to know that teachers are not uncritically teaching cultural values that may themselves be questionable? How are we to know, in other words, that teachers are not merely indoctrinating students into the social rules, conventions, and mores of the culture in the name of creating a common ground for learning? Consider, *Core Knowledge* asserts that they ask teachers "to recognize the needs of each child as part of a larger community. All communities require some common ground. The community of the classroom requires, in particular, that its members share some common knowledge, because this knowledge makes communication and progress in learning possible." It is important to recognize that common knowledge, and common ground are not good in and of themselves. We can *commonly agree* to see the history of our country in a distorted way in order not to face unpleasant truths about our past. We can agree on this *common ground*. But, from an intellectual perspective, we are not justified in doing so. Educated persons would see the problems in this way of thinking and guard against it. There is no shortcut to teachers learning to think critically about and through all content they are expected to teach, at all levels, in all grades. Otherwise indoctrination is all too likely.

Creative Thinking

Essential Idea: Uncreative thinking, thinking that simply repeats old ideas without improving on them, is often a problem in human life. Using the tried — and true does not always work. Standard procedures, old solutions, sometimes break down, sometimes become part of the problem rather than part of the solution. Sometimes it is important to be able to use thinking to *create* (conceive, invent, produce, author) new ideas which enable us to better achieve our purposes or discover new purposes.

Proper Educational Use: It is important to teach in such a way as to encourage students to think for themselves and explore new thoughts and ideas, not just rely on old ones. Students should realize that there are many things which we don't understand and that we often need new and bold ideas. Consequently, those who have emphasized *creative* thinking properly seek strategies and structures which encourage students to use their imaginations to seek nonstandard ways to do standard things, as well as to invent entirely new things that are useful. We need to encourage students to stimulate their creative potential. We need to continually send these types of messages to our students: "Be ready to look at things in new ways. Be ready to seek new paths, invent new ideas, turn things around in different ways. Question standard assumptions, question standard concepts, question what is taken to be acceptable. Be willing to think in unique and different ways. Be a pathfinder, not just a path follower."

Likely Misuse: When "creativity" is not deeply understood, it easily reduces to mere "novelty." And while all genuine creativity produces novelty, not all novelty is genuinely creative. It is easy to produce new *foolish* or *silly* ideas. It is easy to produce what is simply bizarre, strange, or odd. Students' writing is sometimes called creative when it is simply strange or unusual. Teachers who do not understand the important connection between creative and critical thinking often treat them as opposites rather than as conjunctive and complementary. They often inadvertently encourage pseudo creativity rather than genuine creativity. Genuine creativity does not run counter to critical thought, rather it builds upon it and is interwoven with it. Criticality continually heightens our sense of what is inadequate in what we presently do, think, or assume. It points in the direction of, and commonly suggests, what we need to aim at to get a useful new solution. It helps protect us from simply making matters worse. It saves us from running down blind alleys which are simply "new." It enables us to keep our common sense and wits about us.[4]

Critical Thinking

Essential Idea: This basic concept of critical thinking is embedded not only in a core body of research over the last 30 to 50 years but is also derived from roots in ancient Greek. The word 'critical' derives etymologically from two Greek roots: "kriticos" (meaning **discerning judgment**) and "kriterion" (meaning <u>standards</u>). Etymologically, then, the word implies the development

---

4   For a more detailed discussion of the relationship between critical and creative thinking, see: Paul, R. and Elder, L. (2004). *The Thinker's Guide to the Nature and Functions of Critical and Creative Thinking.* Dillon Beach: Foundation for Critical Thinking. www.criticalthinking.org

of "discerning judgment based on standards." In Webster's New World Dictionary, the relevant entry reads "characterized by careful analysis and judgment" and is followed by the gloss: "critical, in its strictest sense, implies an attempt at objective judgment so as to determine both merits and faults." Applied to thinking, then, we might provisionally define critical thinking as thinking that explicitly aims at well-founded judgment and hence utilizes appropriate evaluative standards in the attempt to determine the true worth, merit, or value of something.

The tradition of research into critical thinking reflects the perception that human thinking left to itself often gravitates toward prejudice, overgeneralization, common fallacies, self-deception, rigidity, and narrowness. The critical thinking tradition seeks ways of understanding the mind and then training the intellect so that such errors and distortions of thought are minimized. It assumes that the capacity of humans for good reasoning can be nurtured and developed by an educational process aimed directly at that end. It assumes that sound critical thinking maximizes our ability to solve problems of importance to us by helping us to both avoid common mistakes and proceed in the most rational and logical fashion.

For example, those who think critically typically engage in monitoring, reviewing, and assessing: goals and purposes; the way issues and problems are formulated; the information, data, or evidence presented for acceptance; interpretations of such information, data, or evidence; the quality of reasoning presented or developed, basic concepts or ideas inherent in thinking, assumptions made, implications and consequences that may or may not follow; points of view and frames of reference. In monitoring, reviewing and assessing these intellectual constructs, those who think critically characteristically strive for such intellectual criteria as clarity, precision, accuracy, relevance, depth, breadth, fairness, and logicalness. These modes of thinking help us accomplish the ends we are pursuing.

Critical thinking presupposes intellectual traits, dispositions or virtues in addition to intellectual skills. Not only do critical thinkers, for example, gather accurate information and make sure it is relevant to the question at issue, but they also think *fair-mindedly* in interpreting the information. Critical thinkers not only consider all relevant viewpoints, but they enter each viewpoint using *intellectual empathy* so as to fully understand those viewpoints. In other words, they think with intellectual humility, intellectual integrity, intellectual courage, intellectual perseverance, and so forth in reasoning through issues and problems, so as to ensure that they are thinking at the highest level of quality, that their thinking is reasonable, rational, just, in accordance with the issue, context, situation.

Proper Educational Use: Critical thinking is a universal need in education. It is essential at all grade levels in all subjects. This is true because all learning requires thinking and it is the role of critical thinking to ensure that we are thinking at the highest level of quality, no matter what *content,* issue or problem we are reasoning through. Moreover, it is possible to learn how to think more effectively by learning how to think about one's thinking (independent of the subject or content). And there is no more pressing need than for people to take command of the thinking that is controlling their lives, affecting the lives of others, impacting life on the planet.

It is possible to take command of our thinking precisely because there are universal elements in thinking that we can understand and use to control what and how we think. Whenever we think (and whatever we think about), we think for a purpose within a point of view based on assumptions and leading to implications and consequences. We use data, facts, and experiences to come to conclusions based on concepts and theories in attempting to answer a question, solve a problem, or resolve issues. To illustrate, since all thinking involves purposes and goals, you can always improve your thinking (through critical thinking) by keeping your purposes and goals clearly in mind. Or again, since all thinking requires questions or problems as a central consideration, you can always improve your thinking (through critical thinking) by making sure that you state questions and problems in a precise and accurate way.

If we understand critical thinking substantively, we not only explain the idea explicitly to our students, but we use it to give order and meaning to virtually everything we do as teachers and learners. We use it to organize the design of instruction. It informs how we conceptualize our students as learners. It determines how we conceptualize our role as instructors. It enables us to understand and explain the thinking that defines the content we teach.

When we understand critical thinking at a deep level, we realize that we must teach content through thinking, not content and then thinking. We model the thinking that students need to master if they are to take ownership of the content. We teach history as historical thinking. We teach biology as biological thinking. We teach math as mathematical thinking. We expect students to analyze the thinking that is the content, and then to assess the thinking using intellectual standards. We foster the intellectual traits (dispositions) essential to critical thinking. We teach students to use critical thinking concepts as tools in entering into any system of thought, any subject or discipline. We teach students to construct in their own minds the concepts that define the discipline. We acquire an array of classroom strategies that enable students to master content using their thinking and to become skilled learners.

The concept of critical thinking, rightly understood, ties together much of what we need to understand as teachers and learners, leading to a framework for institutional change.

If we truly understand critical thinking, for example, we should be able to explain its implications:

- for analyzing and assessing reasoning.
- for identifying strengths and weaknesses in thinking.
- for identifying obstacles to rational thought.
- for dealing with egocentrism and sociocentrism.
- for developing strategies that enable one to apply critical thinking to everyday life.
- for understanding the stages of one's development as a thinker.
- for understanding the foundations of ethical reasoning.
- for detecting bias and propaganda in the news.
- for conceptualizing the human mind as an instrument of intellectual work.
- for active and cooperative learning.
- for the art of asking essential questions.
- for scientific thinking.
- for close reading and substantive writing.
- for grasping the logic of a discipline.

Each contextualization in this list is developed in one or more of the Thinker's Guides in the Thinker's Guide Library.[5] Taken together they suggest the robustness of a substantive concept of critical thinking.

In sum, critical thinking defines a network of "invariables" (structures we can use independent of the context) to design integrative, convergent instruction, instruction in which whatever students study is enhanced by everything else they study. We take command of all that is changing in our world, in part by learning how to focus on that which is not changing, and will never change—namely intellectual skills and traits, as well as the universal concepts and principles underlying them. In a world of accelerating change and highly volatile variables, it is only through command of that which does not change that we can acquire powerful tools of learning.

Likely Misuse: There are many problems associated with the use of the term critical thinking in schooling today, and more "pseudo" critical thinking programs than perhaps any other trend. In the first place, virtually all teachers erroneously believe that they understand and practice critical thinking already and that the problem of "uncritical" thinking is fundamentally that of their students (Paul, et al., California Teacher

---

5   See The Thinker's Guides to Critical Thinking, Dillon Beach: Foundation for Critical Thinking Press, www.criticalthinking.org

Preparation, 1997). Secondly, critical thinking is commonly confused with many things that it is not (for example, with cooperative learning, constructivism, Bloom's Taxonomy, the scientific method, common sense, subjective expression of opinions, judgmentalism and negativity, to mention some of the common confusions).

Cultural Literacy

Essential Idea: In his book, *Cultural Literacy* (1987), E.D. Hirsch argues that there is a discrete, relatively small body of specific information possessed by all literate Americans and that this information is the foundation not only of American culture but also the key to literacy and education. Hirsch reasons as follows. Because there is a "descriptive list of the information actually possessed by literate Americans" and because "all human communities are founded upon specific shared information" and because "shared culture requires transmission of specific information to children," it follows that "the basic goal of education in a human community is acculturation." Furthermore, because

> Books and newspapers assume a "common reader" that is a person who knows the things known by other literate persons in the culture… Any reader who doesn't possess the knowledge assumed in a piece he or she reads will in fact be illiterate with respect to that particular piece of writing (p. 13).

In his reasoning, Hirsch links the having of a discrete body of information not only with learning to read but also with becoming educated and indeed with achieving success ("To be culturally literate is to possess the basic information needed to thrive in the modern world.") Hirsch plays down the need for critical thinking and emphasizes instead that the information needed for cultural literacy does not have to be deeply understood:

> The superficiality of the knowledge we need for reading and writing may be unwelcome news to those who deplore superficial learning and praise critical thinking over mere information (p. 15).

The insight that lies behind the idea of cultural literacy is that many communications in a culture presuppose background information, often of a trivial kind. Hence, if someone says "the solution is Mickey Mouse," only those who know who Mickey Mouse will understand what is meant. Based on this view, advocates of cultural literacy often fabricate long lists of terms, sometimes book length in number, that they believe should be directly, though superficially, taught. One consequence is that higher levels of thinking are played down and pretty much left to themselves.

As members of a culture there is no doubt but that we pick up a mass of trivial information that helps us understand the nature of what is going on in the day-to-day life of the culture. The idea behind emphasizing cultural literacy in schooling is the belief that it is possible to accurately formulate a list of essential trivial information and directly teach that information to students, enabling them to effectively decode what is meant by the large mass of communications that surround them and define their worlds.

Proper Educational Use: Given the way cultural literacy is defined by E.D. Hirsch, we can see no proper educational use. Education, properly so called, is not a matter of learning and being able to remember large quantities of disconnected and trivial information.

Likely Misuse: The right way to help students understand and successfully engineer their way through the byways of everyday life in Western mass cultures is a matter of debate. As we said in the section on "core knowledge," those who advocate the model developed by Hirsch make large lists and teach the lists in a didactic way, believing with Hirsch that the key to depth of understanding lies in amassing a large quantity of shallow knowledge. Those who question Hirsch's model question the usefulness of direct didactic teaching of trivial information as a means of achieving cultural literacy. They argue that the most reasonable way to acquire shallow information is through learning powerful (and therefore broad) concepts that are keys to making sense of masses of information. By adopting a framework of critical thinking as a key organizer in developing cultural literacy, one emphasizes the way every dimension of culture is a function of an underlying purpose, involving key concepts and theory, based on a dominant point of view, grounded in foundational assumptions, and having predictable implications and consequences. Students learn to look for the logic of things, for <u>systems</u> at work (rather than fragmented bits and pieces of information). Thus, in a history course focused on critical thinking, the students learn to think historically. They do not become lost in the minutiae of history. They recognize the essence of it--a story told about the past with the goal of shedding light on the present and the emergent future. They would recognize historical thought in the context of their daily lives as they create a story about their past that is making sense of their present and their emergent future.

Or again, if we were teaching a course on contemporary society and seeking to understand modern mass media in the United States using a critical thinking approach, we would not attempt to have students memorize or cram the myriad bits of information about the media into their heads. We would want students to grasp the basic logic of the media. To do this we might explore the media as a product of two overlapping, conflicting forms of power at work: democratic (power in the hands of the people) and plutocratic (power in the hands of the wealthy). We would identify typical conflicts where the interests of the many conflict with the interests of the (wealthy) few. We would notice how these conflicts shed light on many otherwise perplexing phenomena. In the process of studying the various ways in which democracy and plutocracy come into conflict, students would acquire much information about the media, government, wealth, ignorance, propaganda, etc. What is more, the information would add up to something significant. It would not simply come in one ear and go out the other. The advocates of a Hirschian cultural literacy approach do not see this problem or the power of critical thinking in reducing disorder to order, in making information digestible and meaningful. To them, the situation is simple.

As Hirsch puts it:

> Cultural literacy is shallow; true education is deep. But our analysis of reading and learning suggests the paradox that broad, shallow knowledge is the best route to deep knowledge.

We disagree.

Didactic Teaching
(Teaching Content Through Lecture-Based Coverage)

Essential Idea: Content is, by definition, all that is contained in or dealt with in a course of study. Since every subject *contains* a certain quantity of information, concepts, theories, axioms, principles, truths, etc., many teachers have come to believe that students' learning should be measured by how much of what the subject contains they remember or understand at the end of instruction. This belief has been inadvertently reinforced by concepts like Bloom's Taxonomy which implies that students should gain "knowledge" before they achieve "comprehension," thereby confusing "recall" with "knowledge."

Proper Educational Use: Teachers cannot give students information. They cannot pour content into the minds of students through didactic instruction if it is to remain there. Students, if they are to learn content, must work it into their thinking using their thinking. Very short periods of lecture, combined with regular active and disciplined processing on the part of students, can be an effective way to teach initial understanding of content. Teachers might, for example, briefly explain a concept (5-10 minutes) and then have students write down their understanding of the concept—state, elaborate, and give an example of the concept. This might be followed by a reading exercise focused on the concept. Afterwards, teachers might engage students in a Socratic dialogue focused on the concept.

Pitfalls: Those who emphasize the importance of "content" sometimes confuse learning content with memorizing bits and pieces of what is said in lectures or written in a textbook. When content is so understood, it reduces learning to something close to rote memorization. Rote memorization is often ineffective because:

1. it is usually of short duration,
2. it often does not readily translate into intelligent application,
3. it is often a poor indicator of understanding, and
4. it often misleads both student and teacher as to what has really been learned.

It is important to teach in such a way as to encourage students to recognize that all content is nothing more nor less than an established mode of thinking, and that, as a result, one grasps the content as one learns to think in a special way, hence one learns math when one can think mathematically, biology when one can think biologically, geography when one can think geographically.

**When content is appropriately understood,
one recognizes that students learn it best when they:**

1. engage in the thinking that internalizes the content,
2. are held responsible for assessing the thinking they do (as they learn), and
3. have the thinking they need to do regularly modeled for them.

Emotional Intelligence

Essential Idea: In standard educated usage intelligence is understood as the ability to learn or understand from experience or to respond successfully to new experiences. It involves the ability to acquire and retain knowledge. It implies the use of reason in solving problems and directing conduct effectively.

The term emotion is generally used to mean a state of consciousness having to do with the arousal of feelings and is distinguished from other mental states such as cognition, volition, and awareness of physical sensation. Feeling refers to any of the subjective reactions, pleasant or unpleasant, that one may have to a situation.

Therefore, emotional intelligence can be understood as the bringing of intelligence to bear upon emotions. As such, it would involve the use of high level reasoning in dealing with emotions, as well as adjusting emotions to those which are rationally appropriate in context. Moreover it would entail high quality emotions directly resulting from intelligent decision making.

Finally, it would involve nurturing emotional states that support rationality in any of a number of ways.

The concept of emotional intelligence rightfully broadens the traditional view of intelligence from one which involves purely intellectual constructs to one which involves cognition embedded in emotions, attitudes, and passions, and the continual interplay between the affective and the cognitive.

When one recognizes that affective states can be well or poorly grounded in sound thinking and understanding, then one recognizes the possibility of taking action in setting one's emotional (and cognitive) life in order.

Proper Educational Use: It is important to teach in such a way that students discover the powerful role that emotions play in their life as well as the role that thought plays in the emotions they experience. When they understand that there is a continual interplay between what they think and what they feel, they can take better command of both, tracing out how their thoughts are shaping their emotions and how their emotions are shaping their thoughts.

Furthermore, it is important that students come to realize the role of emotions in the life of an intelligent person. Because of the tremendous role of emotions in human life, because emotions influence both thinking and behavior, students must understand that to make intelligent decisions across the domains of one's life, one must take active command of one's emotions.[6]

Likely Misuse: In recent years, the concept of emotional intelligence has received a considerable amount of attention from the popular media, largely due to popularization of the book written by Daniel Goleman entitled *Emotional Intelligence* (1995). Since that time, Goleman has published several books and articles about emotional intelligence and its application to business. And others are jumping on the EI bandwagon. Some researchers believe emotional intelligence is a cognitive skill that can be measured. Others believe it is a combination of abilities and traits. A whole world of thinking (and a whole lot of money) has been created around the concept of emotional intelligence since Goleman's initial popularization of the notion more than a decade ago. For example, there are now self-report measures of emotional intelligence with emotional quotients (EQ) to parallel IQ. One such measure is *The Emotional Intelligence Appraisal* by Bradberry and Greaves (2005). This test purportedly measures the four EI skills from Daniel Goleman's model:

- Self-Awareness
- Self-Management
- Social Awareness
- Relationship Management

6   For more detailed discussion of the relationship between cognition and affect, see Elder, L. and Paul, R. (2007). *The Miniature Guide to the Human Mind*. Dillon Beach, CA: Foundation for Critical Thinking Press. www.criticalthinking.org

However, the original theory of mind presented by Goleman, and consequently his subsequent work, which attempts to explain the relationship between cognition and emotion, contains serious flaws. These flaws result from Goleman's assumption that the relationship between emotions and thoughts is best understood through research into brain functioning. Yet brain research can be both useful and dangerous in helping us understand the mind. There is no easy translation from facts about the brain to facts about the mind. Hence, we must always cross-check such translations by means of our direct experience of our own mind and that of others. For example, Goleman asserts, based on brain research, that emotions often occur before thought. That this is misleading is shown by remembering that for an emotion to be an emotion, it must have some cognitive definition. Hence, fear, as an emotion, presupposes that we have interpreted something (cognitively) as threatening us. Indeed every emotion we experience can be defined cognitively, precisely because there is some thinking which results in or defines that emotion. (of course, we are speaking here of people without severe psychiatric problems. In such people emotions and thoughts may well be disconnected. Note also, that Goleman himself was focused on "normal people").

Moreover, because, in his view, emotions often occur prior to thought, Goleman asserts that emotions are capable of "hijacking" thinking. In other words, emotions are capable of taking over thinking (when the amygdala "hijacks" the neocortex). When this happens, according to Goleman, emotions control the thinking and behavior of the individual. If this is true, how then can a person be held accountable for behavior which results from such "hijacking?" This belief in "emotional hijackings" negates the idea that humans are capable of controlling their emotions and controlling the behavior which results from those emotions. In Goleman's view, it would be reasonable to respond to a question about why I engaged in this or that emotionally charged negative behavior with the explanation, "I just experienced an emotional hijacking." In typical everyday interactions with people, "normal people" are held accountable for their behavior. Excuses like, "I was hijacked by my amygdala. Therefore I couldn't help throwing that plate of food at you" just won't get us very far.

In the time since Goleman's first book on EI was written more than a decade ago, researchers have begun to question his claims about emotional intelligence, and to question how and to what extent, if at all, it can be measured.

The life cycle of the emotional intelligence movement illuminates the typical pattern of fads. First a new "wonderful idea" is born. It is then popularized and spreads. Then people begin to see its weaknesses, its vagueness, its lack of applicability or substance. Then it gradually dies. The fact that researchers are now questioning the emotional intelligence concept as defined by brain-to-mind theoreticians portends its near decline as a superficial, misleading idea. We shall see.

Feminist & Gender Issues

Essential Idea: The call to include the feminist perspective in education is generally based on two primary claims:

1. schools have traditionally been dominated by male-based perspectives to the relative exclusion of female perspectives, and
2. female students think differently from male students and have a right to have their unique mode of thinking acknowledged and emphasized.

Proper Educational Use: There can be no doubt that men have traditionally had far more power in society than women have had. And consequently, thinking that encouraged or justified the male domination of power has traditionally been insinuated in many subtle ways in schooling as well as in the broader society. It is therefore appropriate that educators should closely scrutinize the representations of men and women in school texts, tests, and classroom activities to ensure that gender bias is removed.

On the other hand, it is not at all obvious that there is a *genetic* basis for the claim that men and women "think" differently. This is an issue that has been debated by feminist theoreticians for many years. It may be that whatever general differences existing between the thinking of men and women today are merely a result of differing sex role conditioning. After all, since men and women are still socialized differently, it is likely that to some extent they will think differently. However, since one of the most important goals of education is to aid students in questioning their social conditioning and, hence, to think in broader and more cosmopolitan ways (than persons trapped in narrow social perspectives), it follows that socialized differences should not be reinforced in the classroom. Properly conceived, education should enable us to recognize and transcend ethnocentrism and *in-group* conditioning.

Raising gender based issues in education is fully compatible with the liberating goals of education. At the same time, one must be careful not to favor any "ideology" in the process, whether that ideology be ethnically, socially, racially, or gender based.

Likely Misuse: On occasion, those anxious to correct for male dominated ideologies inadvertently foster an equally unjustified female dominated ideology. Thus, as men, in the past, have tended to portray themselves as superior to women, some women counter with a tendency to present women as superior to men. Education is never well served insofar as *any* ideology is systematically fostered as the *truth* in the classroom. Ideologies, by their nature, typically view the world in selective and one-sided ways (and, by implication, at least somewhat distort the truth). Education should be designed so that all students are encouraged to think for themselves, to come to their own views and perspectives concerning the nature of the world we live in. Presenting conflicting points of view, assigning questions that may be reasoned through from multiple perspectives, and requiring students to empathically role-play perspectives they are unsympathetic to, as well as defending perspectives they are sympathetic to, are all ways to foster open-mindedness and skills essential to the educated mind. Processes such as these, engaged in regularly and routinely in the classroom, teach students to respect the insights of multiple perspectives, without thinking rigidly or narrowly within one view.

Gifted Education

Essential Idea: The general idea behind gifted education programs is that students considered highly talented or advanced in particular domains of thinking, such as in logical/mathematical reasoning, language development, or artistic abilities, need to be provided with *special education* which will further enhance their skills. A basic assumption underlying such programs is that "gifted" students will not be sufficiently challenged, and may become easily bored with normal instruction.

Proper Educational Use: Without question, students' capabilities differ, sometimes greatly, within any given classroom. Therefore some students within any group of students will have more developed skills than others, and the advanced students will be advanced in differing ways. The challenge for teachers, then, is to figure out *how to help all students* develop their capacity to learn and grow intellectually. The best configuration and the best learning occurs when students learn from one another in a classroom wherein the primary focus is the development of student reasoning abilities. In the critical thinking classroom, students are taught to give one another constructive feedback using intellectual standards, and routinely engage in such practice. Even "gifted" students are often weak in understanding how to apply intellectual standards to their reasoning and to the reasoning of others. Yet their reasoning abilities and, in turn, their ability to function well in a complex world, will always depend upon how well they are able to apply these standards.

Thus, in the ideal learning situation, students of varying skill levels routinely learn from one another as they all improve their ability to ask substantive and relevant questions, as well as give high quality feedback such as:

> Could you clarify that statement? I don't understand what you are trying to say. How do you know that what you are saying is accurate? What information did you use to come to that conclusion? What are you assuming? Are you certain that is a sound conclusion? How is that statement relevant to what we are trying to figure out? Is there another plausible way to interpret the situation?

Likely Misuse: There are a number of potential pitfalls in gifted education programs. First, the idea of removing high achieving students from the regular classroom for special programs is riddled with social implications. Such children may be ostracized by other "normal" children. Moreover, "gifted" children may come to the erroneous conclusion that they are more special than other students, that they are smarter simply because special programs are set up for them. They may then come to see "normal" students as inferior to them. In turn "normal" students may see themselves as intellectually inferior to their "gifted" counterparts.

Second, assuming there is good reason to pull students out of regular classrooms because they are "gifted" (which is not necessarily a justifiable assumption), there are no guarantees that these students will be more intellectually challenged than they would be in the regular classroom. Simply setting up a special program in no way ensures high quality learning. Rather, *the quality of learning is directly dependent upon the quality of the teachers' thinking within the program.*

Third, some "gifted" students have great potential for developing their minds only to the extent that they become successful, manipulating, and controlling adults. In other words, they learn to think critically for the purpose of serving their selfish interests. Through high level intellectual skills they become especially adept at self-deception and rationalization. Therefore any "gifted" education program must include an ethical component so that students learn how to engage in high quality reasoning *that also takes into account the rights and needs of others.* Put another way, students considered "quick" learners frequently more naturally develop their intellectual capacities than students who struggle with learning. Learning is easier in many ways for them because they are born with the intellectual "hardware" that others may not have. But it doesn't follow that they will also develop ethical propensities at the same time they are developing their intellectual capacities. The result is often the development of selfish, or *weak-sense* critical thinking. These people often gain positions of power due to their natural intellectual prowess. They are adept at intellectual sophistry, at manipulation, at gaining power and control at the expense of others' rights and needs. It is vitally important, therefore, that gifted education programs actively foster the development of fair-minded, or *strong-sense*, critical thinking.

Global Education

Essential Idea: The essential idea behind global education is that we are increasingly living in a "global" world, a world in which business competition comes fundamentally from a global economy that must be understood from a global perspective, a world in which our well-being is linked with the well-being of other peoples around the world, and an ecological environment which must be understood in terms of global systems and forces. The basic premise is that if we school our citizens in a parochial manner, they will not be able to serve the country, the economy, or themselves in a productive way. From this point of view, our survival is linked to the degree to which we learn to teach and think in global terms.

Proper Educational Use: In global education the curriculum is designed through a global perspective. Problems are introduced into the curriculum that involve facts, concepts, and issues that cut across national and cultural boundaries. In global education, students must learn to think within complex international systems, in terms of systems within systems, to think within cultural, ecological, political, economic, and technological systems and their interrelationships. This ensures that students will have to think through many complex issues involving multiple perspectives and virtually unlimited data. Most of these issues require that students learn to deal effectively with multiple sources of conflicting data, multiple interpretations of significant realities, and multiple interests competing for limited resources.

Likely Misuse: Most teachers have not themselves been globally educated, and hence are not prepared to teach from a global perspective. Secondly, and most importantly, one cannot think properly from a global perspective without thinking critically and, of course, most teachers have not been well-prepared to think critically. The result is that most programs of global education will be fundamentally "window dressing" rather than substantial. Only those programs linked with long-term staff development in critical thinking and global issues offer a plausible hope of success.

Inquiry-Based Teaching

Essential Idea: The principle idea behind inquiry-based teaching is that all disciplines are based in specific methods for gathering information, interpreting that information, and generating solutions to problems. Working from this assumption, advocates of inquiry-based teaching emphasize that students learn a subject best by engaging in the modes of inquiry characteristic of that discipline. The classroom is then viewed as a setting in which inquiry should be the dominant focus. Students should be taught how to engage in the basic methods of inquiry used within a discipline and they should spend the bulk of their time doing so. Through this process, it is assumed that students will learn the real operational meanings of key concepts and principles in the field. Often inquiry-based approaches utilize *cases* or typical *problems* within the discipline as the stimulus for inquiry.

Proper Educational Use: The notion that one learns chemistry by doing chemistry, math by doing math, history by doing history is sound. And insofar as there are characteristic ways in which different disciplines gather information, define questions, and pursue answers, students ought to learn and use them in studying a subject. Designing instruction in this spirit is essential to deeply internalizing a subject.

Likely Misuse: The danger is that teachers will teach an oversimplified version of inquiry. This is likely to happen when teachers do not understand the basic logic of the discipline they teach. To teach effectively using an inquiry-based approach, teachers must understand and have command of the elements of reasoning that define the discipline they are teaching. When teachers understand these fundamental structures, they recognize that all subjects, all disciplines, have a fundamental logic defined by the structures of thought embedded in them.

To lay bare a subject's most fundamental logic, teachers should begin with these questions:

- What is the main **purpose** or **goal** of studying this subject? What are people in this field trying to accomplish?
- What kinds of **questions** do they ask? What kinds of problems do they try to solve?
- What sorts of **information** or data do they gather?
- What types of **inferences** or judgments do they typically make?
- How do they go about gathering information in ways that are distinctive to this field?
- What are the most basic ideas, **concepts** or theories in this field?
- What do professionals in this field take for granted or **assume**?
- What **viewpoint** is fostered in this field?
- What **implications** follow from studying this discipline? How are the products of this field used in everyday life?

In short, true inquiry cannot be taught as mechanical procedural thinking. Sound inquiry requires critical thinking. It requires that students learn the basic structures of thought (purpose, question, information, interpretation, concept, assumption, implication, and point of view) as well as the fundamental intellectual standards (clarity, precision, accuracy, relevance, depth, breadth, logicalness, and significance).

Intelligence

Essential Idea: Intelligence implies the ability to learn or understand from experience or to respond successfully to new situations or, put another way, the ability to reason well in solving problems, directing conduct, and making judgments. In this broad sense, the development of intelligence is none other than the fundamental goal of education. The traditional use of the word in psychology, in contrast, is often much more narrow, often treating "intelligence" as equivalent to a score on a particular test emphasizing certain kinds of verbal, mathematical, or spatial judgments. In this narrow sense of the word, intelligence is assumed to be a more or less unchangeable collection of innate capacities (and limitations) of a particular person's brain. Fortunately, at least some psychologists are moving toward a broader use of the term.[7] Nevertheless, some still consider it as something more or less unchangeable in the lifetime of a person.

Proper Educational Use: It is important to teach so as to encourage students to learn from experience and to respond successfully to new situations in their lives. Certainly, students need to learn to reason well in solving problems, directing conduct, and making judgments about the events, circumstances, and direction of their lives. It is important to recognize that students can develop their ability to learn from experience, that they can develop their ability to reason well and solve problems in their everyday and professional lives. Understood in this sense intelligence is something we can develop, for clearly it is possible to learn how to learn from experience. When students learn how to think critically, they develop their ability to reason well in solving problems, directing conduct, and making judgments.

Likely Misuse: It is easy to lose perspective concerning the appropriate meaning of the word "intelligence," especially since it is being used in the field of psychology in such a multiplicity of ways. If one does not keep clearly in mind the broad sense of "intelligence," and teach with that broad sense in mind, one can easily foster a more narrow talent or preferred way to learn at the expense of the broad foundational abilities every person needs to function well in the world.

Integrated Curriculum

Essential Idea: It is common for instruction and learning to be highly fragmented. When they are, students fail to see how ideas are connected to other ideas in systems (which are themselves connected to other systems). When students learn content in bits and pieces as if they were separate items

---

7   For a more detailed discussion of the limitations of intelligence tests in assessing intelligence, see Howe, M. 1997. *IQ in Question: The Truth About Intelligence*. Thousand Oaks, CA: Sage Publications.

to memorize, they tend to forget them quickly, to misunderstand them, and to be ineffective in transferring them to new contexts. With this problem in mind, many educators have attempted to develop "integrated" curriculum. The idea is to find ways to make connections among ideas explicit to teachers (as they plan their instruction) and to students (as they learn).

Proper Educational Use: Since all disciplines represent ways of thinking, and all thinking presupposes common elements and standards, integration can be achieved through an emphasis on critical thinking. When history is taught as historical thinking, biology as biological thinking, geography as geographical thinking, students begin to see deep connections between these subjects, as well as important connections within them. When students are taught that all human activity presupposes human thinking, and that all thinking has common parts and can be evaluated using common standards, the door is opened for them to begin to take charge of their learning (by beginning to take charge of their thinking). In science, students learn to think scientifically. While reading, they learn to think like a good reader. When listening, they learn to listen well. They consider purposes, how they pose problems, what information they are using, how they are interpreting that information, what concepts they are using, what they are assuming, what they are implying, from what point of view they are reasoning, whether they are being clear or vague, accurate or inaccurate, precise or imprecise, relevant or irrelevant, logical or illogical, etc. They reason in this way in all of their subject areas and carry it out into their personal lives as well. What is my central goal? What problems am I facing? What information do I need to effectively address this problem?

There are many additional ways to articulate the proper *integration of curriculum*. Consider for example the relationship between substantive writing, learning systems of meanings, and relating core ideas to other core ideas. To gain knowledge, we must construct it in our minds. Writing what we are trying to internalize helps us achieve that purpose. When we are able to make connections in writing, we begin to take ownership of these connections. To do this, we must learn how to identify core ideas in the books we read and then explain those ideas, along with the role they play within the subjects we are studying, in writing.

All knowledge exists in systems of meanings, with interrelated primary, secondary, and peripheral ideas. Imagine a series of circles beginning with a small core circle of primary ideas, surrounded by concentric circles of secondary ideas and an outer circle of peripheral ideas. The primary ideas at the core explain the secondary and peripheral ideas. Whenever we read to acquire knowledge, we must write to take ownership, first of the primary ideas, for they are key to understanding all the other ideas. Furthermore, just as we must write to gain an initial understanding of the primary ideas, we must also write to begin to think within the system as a whole and to make interconnections between ideas. The sooner we begin to think, and therefore write, within a system, the sooner the system becomes meaningful to us.

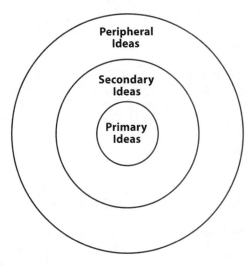

Essential Idea:
Writing about primary
and secondary ideas
in a discipline is a
key to understanding
the discipline.

Thus, when we take command of a core of historical ideas, we begin to think and write historically. When we take command of a core of scientific ideas, we begin to think and write scientifically. Core or primary ideas are the key to every system of knowledge. They are the key to learning any subject. They are the key to retaining what we learn and applying it to life's problems. Until we write about these ideas, they never fully take root in our minds. But by seeking out these ideas and digesting them, we multiply the important subjects we can write about, as well as the important things we can say about them.

We should use writing to relate core ideas we learn within one discipline or domain to core ideas in other systems of knowledge, for knowledge exists not only in a system but also in relation to other systems of knowledge. Mastering any set of foundational ideas makes it easier to learn other foundational ideas. Learning to think within one system of knowledge helps us learn within other systems. Writing is crucial to that process.

For example, if in studying botany we learn that all plants have cells, we should connect this idea to the fact that all animals have cells (which we learned in studying biology). We then can begin to consider the similarities and differences between the types of animal and plant cells while recognizing a foundational concept that applies to both botany and biology. Or consider the relation between psychology and sociology. Psychology focuses on individual behavior while sociology focuses on group behavior. But people's individual psychology influences how they relate to group norms, and social groups shape how individuals deal with their perceived life problems and opportunities. By putting core ideas within these two disciplines into words, we better understand both fields and therefore can more effectively apply our knowledge to the real world (wherein the psychological and sociological are deeply intertwined).[8]

Likely Misuse: Unfortunately, very few educators have studied the structure of the disciplines in such a way as to understand the deeper connections which make significant integration possible. The result is often that superficial connections are used in place of deeper ones, and the goal of integrated learning fails. Students cannot build important learnings on superficial connections.

Learning Styles

Essential Idea: It is often believed that most people favor some particular method of taking in and processing information and stimuli. Based on this concept, the idea of individualized "learning styles" originated in the 1970s, and has gained popularity in recent years. A *learning style* is the method of learning particular to an individual that presumably leads that individual to learn best. Teachers who use a learning styles approach in teaching typically attempt to assess the learning styles of their students and adapt their classroom methods to best fit each student's learning style. More than 80 learning styles models have been proposed.

One popular type of model often includes four basic learning styles:

- Visual Learning (learn by seeing)
- Auditory Learning (learn by hearing)
- Reading/Writing (learn by processing text)
- Kinesthetic or Practical Learning (learn by doing)

Aiming to explain why aptitude tests, school grades, and classroom performance often fail to identify real ability, Robert J. Sternberg listed various "cognitive dimensions" in his book *Thinking Styles* (1997). Several other models are also often used when researching learning styles, most commonly the Myers-Briggs Type Indicator and Howard Gardner's Multiple Intelligence Model.

---

8   For further discussion of the important role of writing in learning, see Paul, R. and Elder, L. (2006). *The Thinker's Guide to How to Write a Paragraph: The Art of Substantive Writing.* Dillon Beach, CA: Foundation for Critical Thinking Press. www. criticalthinking.org

Proper Educational Use: Given what can be commonly observed in the classroom, it stands to reason that some students learn more easily when exposed to certain types of learning aids or when certain learning processes are used in teaching. For example, it is possible that some students learn more readily through *visual* stimuli than through other modes of input. This might be true, for example, for students with particular learning disabilities (when they have trouble reading, they might more readily understand what they see in pictures, for instance). Similarly, some students might be more outspoken or extraverted in class while others might be more introverted. When this is the case, teachers may need to figure out ways to bring all students more equally into the learning process. Thus *basic and fundamental* ways of using the concept of learning styles might be useful in the classroom.

Likely Misuse: It is important to recognize that many scholars have critiqued learning styles theories during the past several decades. Some psychologists and neuroscientists have questioned the scientific basis for these models and the theories on which they are based. Many educational psychologists believe there is little evidence for the efficacy of most learning styles models, and furthermore that the models often rest on dubious theoretical grounds (Curry, 1990). According to Stahl (2002), there has been an "utter failure to find that assessing children's learning styles and matching to instructional methods has any effect on their learning." A literature review by authors from the University of Newcastle upon Tyne identified 71 different theories of learning style. This report, published in 2004, criticized most of the main instruments used to identify an individual's learning style. Given the growing body of critique focused on learning styles, on what they are, and how they are to be measured, it seems prudent to use any learning styles theory with caution.

In any case, when employing learning styles theories, *teachers should never lose track of what makes for an educated person.* All educated persons in today's world, for example do and must learn to read, and to read well. Though students may be visual learners, still they must learn to read closely, to deeply understand important ideas illuminated in written work. Though looking at pictures might assist them in learning to read, still at some point students must learn to decipher and work their way through texts of written form (though this may well be a frustrating process). Similarly, though students may be introverted, still they must learn to articulate their views intelligently. We impede their learning when we allow them to sit quietly in the classroom under the label of "introverted learning style."

As educators, teachers are obligated to bring every student into the learning process as intimately as possible and to foster deep learning through content. This presupposes that teachers understand what it means to be an educated person and can foster the skills necessary for bringing this about.

In sum, teachers do students an injustice when we pander to their "learning style" at the expense of their becoming educated persons. Learning styles theory cannot be allowed to impede the process of cultivating the intellect.

Multiculturalism

Essential Idea: Students should learn that there are many cultures in the world and that all cultures are worth understanding and respecting for their positive attributes and achievements. They should recognize that it makes no sense to make sweeping judgments, good or bad, about cultures as a whole. They should recognize that it is common, but not justified, for people to see their own culture as intrinsically superior to other cultures (the problem of ethnocentricity). They should learn that we can learn things of significance from all cultures.

Proper Educational Use: In fostering *multicultural* awareness, teachers should stress the need for properly evaluating aspects of cultures, especially those aspects with an ethical dimension. Some culturally common practices violate basic human rights. For example, some cultures treat women as inferior to men or treat some social groups within their culture as superior to others. Some cultures systematically teach people that this or that group is inferior or "tainted" in some way and should be shunned or treated with disdain. Students cannot learn to deal rationally with the multiplicity of cultures in the world without thinking critically about the concept of "culture," about specific practices within cultures, about how any given culture can simultaneously foster both high achievement and indefensible practices.

Cultural diversity derives from the fact that there are an unlimited number of alternative ways for social groups to satisfy their needs and desires. Yet, traditional ways of living within a social group or culture take on the force of habit and custom. They are handed down from one generation to another. To the individuals in a given group they seem to be the *only* way, or the only *reasonable* way, to do things. And these social customs sometimes have ethical implications. Social habits and customs answer questions like this:

- How should marriage take place? Who should be allowed to marry, under what conditions, and with what ritual or ceremony? Once married what role should the male(s), if any, play? What role should the female(s), if any, play? Are multiple marriage partners possible? Is divorce possible? Under what conditions?

- Who should care for the children? What should they teach the children as to proper and improper ways to act? When children do not act as they are expected to, how should they be treated?

- When should children be accepted as adults? When should they be considered old enough to be married? Who should they be allowed to marry?

- Given that children have natural sensual and even sexual desires from a very early age, how should children be allowed to act on those desires (if at all)? With whom, if anyone, should they be allowed to engage in sexual exploration and discovery? What sexual acts are considered acceptable and wholesome? What sexual acts are considered perverted or sinful?

- How should men and women dress? To what degree should their body be exposed in public? How is nudity treated? How are those who violate these codes treated?

- How should food be obtained and how should it be prepared? Who is responsible for obtaining food? Who for preparing it? How should it be served? How eaten?

- How is the society stratified (into levels of power)? How is the society controlled? What belief system is used to justify the distribution of scarce goods and services and the way rituals and practices are carried out?

- If the society is threatened from without, how will it deal with those threats? How will it defend itself? How does the society engage in war, or does it?

- What sorts of games, sports, or amusements will be practiced in the society? Who is allowed to engage in them?

- What religions are taught or allowable within the society? Who is allowed to participate in the religious rituals or to interpret divine or spiritual teachings to the group?

- How are grievances settled in the society? Who decides who is right and who wrong? How are violators treated?

Note that many of the questions above illuminate social practices that are merely a matter of personal group choice, while others have ethical implications. For any action to be unethical, it must inherently deny another person or creature some inalienable right. Based on this definition, the following classes of acts are unethical in-and-of-themselves, whether any particular culture engages in them, whether any particular culture attempts to justify them under the guise of "their particular viewpoint." Thus any person or group that violates them is properly criticized from an ethical standpoint:

- **Slavery:** Owning people, whether individually or in groups.
- **Genocide:** Systematically killing with the attempt to eliminate a whole nation or ethnic group.
- **Torture:** Inflicting severe pain, physical or psychological, to force information, get revenge or serve some other irrational end.
- **Sexism:** Treating people unequally (and harmfully) in virtue of their gender.

- **Racism:** Treating people unequally (and harmfully) in virtue of their race or ethnicity.

- **Murder:** The pre-meditated killing of people for revenge, pleasure, or to gain advantage for oneself.

- **Assault:** Attacking an innocent person with intent to cause grievous bodily harm.

- **Rape:** Forcing an unwilling person to have intercourse.

- **Fraud:** Intentional deception that causes someone to give up property or some right.

- **Deceit:** Representing something as true which one does not know to be true.

- **Intimidation:** Forcing persons to act against their interest or deterring them from acting in their interest by threats of violence.

- Putting persons in jail without telling them the charges against them or providing them with a reasonable opportunity to defend themselves.

- Putting persons in jail, or otherwise punishing them, solely for their views.

One important problem in teaching "multiculturalism" is that teachers often inadvertently foster confusion between social conventions and ethics because they themselves are unable to distinguish between these two very different modes of thinking. Because teachers and administrators have largely internalized the conventions of society the schools traditionally function as apologists for conventional thought. Education, properly so called, should foster the intellectual skills that enable students to distinguish between cultural mores and ethical precepts, between social commandments and ethical truths. In each case, when social beliefs and taboos conflict with ethical principles, ethical principles should prevail. These important understandings, therefore, must lie at the heart of any multicultural program.

Likely Misuse: To effectively foster a rich concept of multiculturalism, and to avoid yet another form of indoctrination, teachers must be able to distinguish true ethics from social conventions, taboos and rules. They must understand the difference between what people are obligated to do and what society merely expects them to do in the name of tradition. Without this distinction, what is merely group preference can be easily mistaken for ethical (or unethical) behavior.[9]

In other words, when "culture" is *not* properly understood, "multiculturalism" easily reduces to "political correctness" or mere empty praise of all cultures. It is easy to get students to mindlessly praise all cultures without achieving any deep understanding of any culture. It is more challenging to help students recognize that there are many cultures in the world, each with achievements

---

9   For a more detailed explanation of the distinction between ethics and social conventions, see Paul, R. And Elder, L (2006). *The Thinker's Guide to Understanding the Foundations of Ethical Reasoning.* Dillon Beach, CA: Foundation for Critical Thinking Press. www.criticalthinking.org

and failures, each with admirable characteristics as well as weaknesses or problems that need to be analyzed and addressed.

Multiple Intelligences

Essential Idea: The essential idea of *multiple intelligences* is that the traditional idea of intelligence must be broadened beyond the standard verbal/mathematical form of intelligence, to include a number of intellectual, artistic, and physical domains within which human beings are capable of excelling and should be encouraged to excel. Students should be encouraged to develop those "intelligences" that interest them and that they are naturally inclined toward.

Proper Educational Use: If we understand the concept of multiple intelligences to mean the many domains of human thought within which any student might excel or be interested in, it is important to teach in such a way that students learn to develop them. Indeed students should excel in as many important domains of thought as they are capable of, and to some extent they should excel in those domains toward which they are drawn. Certainly, we must broaden our view of what it means to be intelligent beyond the narrow focus on skill areas traditionally measured by intelligence tests.

In standard educated usage "intelligence" is understood as the ability to learn or understand from experience or to respond successfully to new experiences. It involves the ability to acquire and retain knowledge. It implies the use of reason in solving problems and directing conduct effectively.

Given this definition of "intelligence," multiple intelligences would thus roughly mean the ability to learn or understand from experience in multiple domains, or to respond successfully to new experiences in multiple domains.

Because students are likely to face a variety of complex problems in many different intellectual fields throughout their lives, they must develop multiple intelligences for successful functioning within those fields. For example, students must learn to reason well through economic, sociological, historical, scientific, and mathematical questions. They must learn to deal responsibly with their emotions. They must learn to scrutinize their behavior in order to upgrade it. They must understand the role of self-deception in thinking. Thus students must have intellectual command over all of these domains, and many others, to function well, broadly speaking. Therefore it makes sense to foster the development of multiple intelligences.

However, the skills students need to successfully think through these domains are *generalizable*, intellectual tools which enable students to develop such "multiple intelligences," as well as to develop new "intelligences."

Likely Misuse: When the concept of multiple intelligences is misused in the classroom, one fundamental pitfall is that teachers consider every "intelligence" as equally important and largely a matter of personal preference. But there are important skills and abilities for students to learn, no matter what is easier or more "fun" for them. To some extent students should be encouraged to develop within the domains which interest them. Yet education, properly so called, has as its first obligation to teach students intellectual command over their minds, to teach students the intellectual skills they must have to function well in their world. To elaborate, students need to learn how to pursue intellectual questions, how to clarify and evaluate purposes, how to check information for accuracy and relevance, how to uncover faulty assumptions, how to think through issues of conflict in a fair-minded way, how to follow out the implications of this decision versus that decision, how to consider multiple possible conclusions to a problem, how to think through their use of concepts to ensure they are using these concepts justifiably. To function in the world they face, students will need highly developed skills in reading, writing and oral communication. *These skills are not a choice, but a necessary condition for effectively living in a highly complex world.*

If teachers are using Howard Gardner's theory of multiple intelligences as a guide to instructional practices, they are emphasizing development of the following "intelligences" as delineated by Gardner:

1. Language
2. Logical-mathematical analysis
3. Spatial representation
4. Musical thinking
5. Kinesthetic thinking
6. Self-knowledge
7. Understanding of others
8. Naturalistic
9. Existential (which Gardner adds as a possibility)

If we interpret Gardner's theory to mean that people excel in different categories of thought, the theory can have some use. But to say that these categories characterize "intelligences" per se may not be the best conceptualization. Since Gardner's theory was published in 1983 (*Frames of Mind: The Theory of Multiple Intelligences*), it has been widely criticized in the psychology and educational theory communities. The most common criticisms argue that Gardner's theory is based on his own intuition rather than empirical data and that the "intelligences" are just talents or personality types under another name.

Whether Gardner's theory is problematic in and of itself, the manner in which it is embodied in the classroom often is. Certainly Gardner's list of *intelligences*, as well as many other potential intelligences, could be identified. Yet, again, emphasis on any one of them in the classroom must be driven by the ultimate goals of education. In other words, if our role as educators is to teach students the intellectual skills they will need to make reasonable, rational decisions as adults, then we must emphasize development of the *intelligences* which result in their ability to do so. For example, there is no getting around the fact that it is far more important for students to learn to evaluate their thinking, to effectively assess it, and to upgrade it when reasoning through complex issues than it is to pursue musical or kinesthetic inclinations. When we have provided the intellectual foundations presupposed in an educated person, we can then afford to focus on less important, but nevertheless interesting, cognitive propensities.

Teachers often emphasize certain "intelligences" in the classroom based on areas of student interest. While we want learning to be fun for students wherever possible, it is often the case that the most important concepts for them to learn are also the most difficult to learn. If we encourage students only toward those "intelligences" they find to be the most interesting, we may inadvertently fail to provide them with the fundamentals essential to the educated mind.

No Child Left Behind

Essential Idea: The No Child Left Behind Act of 2001 (Public Law 107-110), is a United States federal law (signed on January 8, 2002) that reauthorizes federal programs aiming to improve the quality of U.S. primary and secondary schools by increasing accountability. In addition, it provides parents more flexibility in choosing schools their children can attend. What is more, it puts an increased focus on reading and re-authorizes the Elementary and Secondary Education Act of 1965 (ESEA). NCLB is the latest federal law based on the idea that high expectations and setting of goals will result in greater success for all students. Finally, the act requires that schools distribute the name, home phone number and address of every student to military recruiters.

Under this act the progress of all students is to be measured annually in math and reading in grades 3 through 8 and at least once during high school. By the end of the 2007-2008 school year, testing is to be conducted in science once during grades 3–5, 6–9, and 10–11.

Proper Educational Use: There are multiple layers in the NCLB Act, so we will comment here only on one aspect: the claim that it leads to more substantive learning. The proper use of any law such as this is to take advantage of the (albeit limited) funding it provides to develop substantive changes in instruction, with the view that if students are learning to think in a more proficient way, all of the test scores will rise and the students' best interest will have been served. True accountability is compatible with substantive approaches to teaching and learning and such approaches serve every student capable of learning substantively. We might, however, question the extent to which standardized tests are the best educational assessment methods (some would argue that *authentic* or *portfolio assessments* are far superior, for example).

Likely Misuse: The overwhelming focus on standardized testing is likely to result in "teaching to the test," that is, teachers teaching a narrow subset of skills with a view of increasing test performance rather than achieving deeper understanding across multiple contexts and subjects. Moreover, because each state can produce its own standardized tests, states might compensate for inadequate education programs by making the standardized tests so easy that passing them is meaningless.

Schools are also held liable and threatened with sanctions for students who cannot achieve adequately, including those in mentally handicapped classes. This may mean either:

1. that standards will be set too low in order to accommodate special needs students, or
2. that these students will be held to unreasonably high standards, and thus teachers will spend an inordinate amount of time "teaching to the test."

Either of these problems will result in special needs students, who already begin at a disadvantage, failing to learn the skills of thinking they so desperately need to function in the world they will face.

Moreover, NCLB's exclusive focus on math, reading and science scores is likely to have adverse consequences for students in poorly performing schools, as it most likely will narrow a school's emphasis from a potentially broad and rich concept of education to one focused fundamentally on elevating scores on just two or three indicators. It will not be uncommon for many weeks (if not most of the year) to be spent in "teaching to the test."

Outcome-Based Education
(or Standards-Based Education)

Essential Idea: The idea behind outcome-based education is, at root, a simple one. If students are not presently learning what they should know and be able to do, why not focus instruction directly on what they should know and be able to do? When we do, we have outcome-based education. In this sense, when 19th Century elite schools focused instruction on students learning to read classic texts in Latin and Greek, and proficiency in these subjects was the intended "outcome," then they were engaged in outcome-based education.

In the US, outcome-based education has come to mean *objective measurement of student performance*. Measurement may be used to determine whether or not the education system is performing adequately, and in some cases whether or not students will be certified as educated by the system. It is also may be known as Standards-Based Education reform, Mastery Education, systemic education restructuring, Performance-Based Education, High Performance Learning, Total Quality Management, Transformational Education, Competency-Based Education, and Break-the-Mold Schools. It is now primarily focused on setting universal standards requiring students to demonstrate what they know and are able to do (at each grade level and before they can graduate from high school).

Outcome, or Standards-Based, Education, as currently conceptualized in K-12 schooling, calls for restructuring which includes creation of a specific curriculum framework, as well as specific assessments that gauge whether a student falls short of, meets or exceeds the standard (rather than a rank order or letter grade). It links awarding of diplomas, for example, to achieving a particular level on such an assessment. Standards-Based Education is based on the belief that all children can excel or succeed, despite differences in socioeconomic level, gender, language challenges, ethnicity, learning or physical disabilities, etc., and that all students can learn and meet set standards in all subjects.

The best known and most far-reaching standards-based education law in the U.S. is the *No Child Left Behind Act*, which mandates certain measurements for all schools that receive federal education funds. Various consequences for schools failing to make adequate yearly progress are included in the law.

One important final point about the current conceptualization of *Outcome* or *Standards-Based Education* is that it is patterned after the idea of Total Quality Management (TQM), which goes something like this: Schools are like factories. They turn out "products," all of which should be able to do the same (specific and measurable) things, and which should function at the same (or at least minimum) level of quality. Therefore schools, like factories, should focus on "quality control" among students. If outcomes are specified and easily measurable, then processes of *continual improvement* (a TQM term) should make it as easy to produce defect-free students as to produce any other defect-free "product."

Proper Educational Use: Whenever educators design instruction, it is simply good common sense to reflect on what they desire to "produce," as a result. If they are not clear about the ultimate ends of education, they cannot adjust the means to it. Furthermore, it makes sense to create assessment tools that measure the behavior you are hoping to foster and to build accountability into the educational process.

Likely Misuse: Outcome or Standards-Based education, as currently conceptualized in K-12 schooling, is premised in the following:

1. that it is possible to clearly delineate and agree upon the skills, abilities and behaviors we need to foster in schooling.
2. that all students can successfully achieve the standards set for them.
3. that the threat of punishment is a reasonable and effective deterrent for ensuring that schools work toward student achievement in the outcomes set for them (as in the *No Child Left Behind Act*).

It hardly seems plausible that threat of punishment through law will lead to true education, to the development of the intellect, which should be the primary objective of schooling and is the only defensible goal of schooling in a democratic society.   Certainly such threats are justifiable, if at all, only when the standards for which we are holding schools accountable are those that cultivate the educated mind. Since few administrators or teachers have a rich, substantive concept of education, it is unlikely that any Standards-Based reform movement designed by them would advance this concept.

Moreover, it is doubtful whether threat of punishment is effective in the Standards or Outcome-Based Education reform movement in compelling schools to foster student achievement of articulated standards. It is more likely that it leads to the employment of data input, manipulation, analysis and reporting that ensures continued funding (regardless of the level of actual achievement).

Whether or to what extent students can successfully achieve standards set for them depends on a number of complex and interactive variables, including the standards themselves, how they are fostered in the classroom, and the ability or disability levels of students, to name a few. It is of course absurd to think that all students can learn at the same level of quality, as any good teacher knows.

But most important, the success of any Standards-Based approach will depend primarily upon the standards themselves and how teachers foster student learning of those standards. Standards are neither good nor bad in and of themselves. Before supporting any Standards-Based approach, the primary question we should ask is: To what extent does this approach foster the skills, abilities, and traits of the educated mind? And before we attempt to answer this question, we need to ask: What are the skills, abilities and traits of the educated mind? The connection between education and critical thinking is important in answering this last question, as the tools of critical thinking are essential to education. Critical thinking provides the *vehicle* for developing the mind intellectually (through the routine analysis, assessment and improvement of thinking), and is presupposed for thinking well within any field, subject or discipline. In short, critical thinking fosters the skills, abilities and dispositions embodied in the educated mind.

Phonics vs. Whole Language

Essential Idea: These two ideas are based on competing notions of how best to teach young children word recognition skills (and ultimately how to read). The essential idea behind "phonics" is the claim that it is possible and useful to teach students how to sound out words in learning to read. This can be done by focusing on words and their constituent sounds and syllables individually, outside of any particular context. The essential idea behind a "whole language" approach to reading and the recognition of words is the claim that it is easier and more natural for children to learn to recognize individual words not by sounding them out in the absence of context, but rather by putting them together into meaningful patterns in a natural context of use.

Proper Educational Use: It seems clear that there are advantages and disadvantages to both approaches and that they should probably be viewed in terms of the tools they provide teachers. Some amount of time should be spent in learning letter/sound correspondences, especially for students who struggle with learning to decipher words. But time also needs to be spent in speaking words in context, seeing them in context, and writing them in context. To some extent, the issue is analogous to the question of whether it makes sense for beginning tennis players to practice individual strokes against the backboard or gain experience trying to integrate those strokes in the natural context of a full-fledged tennis match. In tennis, of course, the answer is clear. Both practice at the backboard and engagement in actual games are useful.

Pitfall: The fundamental danger that comes from the clash of these two competing theories of how children best learn to recognize and use words is that enthusiasts for either approach tend to put the case into an either/or question (either we use phonics or we use whole language) when it is probably best to put it into a both/and question.

Portfolio-Based or Alternative Assessment

Essential Idea: Alternative or portfolio assessment is in direct contrast to traditional assessment (which includes standardized tests, grades, multiple choice tests, etc.) Alternative assessment is also known under various other terms, including:

- authentic assessment
- integrative assessment
- holistic assessment
- assessment for learning
- formative assessment

In this model, students, teachers, and sometimes parents select pieces from a student's combined work over a designated number of years of school to demonstrate that significant learning and improvement has taken place during those years. The portfolio assessment presumably demonstrates active internalization of knowledge. It is used for evaluating learning processes and outcomes. Alternative assessments are used to encourage student involvement in their own assessment, as well as interaction with other students, teachers, parents and the larger community.

Formats vary. Demonstrations and journals can be used as alternative assessments, while portfolio presentations are considered the most wholly representative of a student's learning.

Proper Educational Use: The premise behind portfolio, alternative, or authentic assessment is that students should, through portfolios created over several years, be able to demonstrate deep and important learning, that these assessments are more likely than traditional measures to show whether and to what extent students are learning content in a meaningful way. As portfolios generally require writing and application of ideas, and as the act and process of writing generally leads to learning at some level and in some form, it seems likely that this form of assessment has merit over traditional measures (such as measures associated with didactic instruction). And portfolios require application of concepts learned to actual contexts, which also is desirable. However, the main question is this: What is the quality of the content being learned and how is it being learned (and demonstrated in these portfolios)?

The quality of portfolio assessment will be only as good as the teaching and learning that results in the portfolio. Students can write extensively about superficial ideas. Students can "learn" and apply ideas without regard to the intellectual standards of clarity, accuracy, logic, depth, breadth, relevance, fairness and so forth. And those assessing portfolios without grounding in critical thinking concepts and principles cannot be expected to do so adequately.

The questions we need to ask in evaluating portfolio assessments include:

1. What is the quality of the content being learned and how is that content being learned?

2. Are students learning to think through the content using discipline and rigor, or are they given free reign to think what they want within the content?

3. To what extent do the portfolios demonstrate that students are learning to think scientifically, to think historically, to think within social studies, to think mathematically, to think within important ideas in literature, to think within any subject or discipline?

4. To what extent do the portfolios demonstrate students' abilities to reason within multiple conflicting viewpoints?

5. To what extent are students learning to take command of their *purposes*, the *questions* they ask which guide the inquiry process, the *information* they use in their reasoning, the *inferences* they make about that information, the *concepts* that are guiding their thinking, the *assumptions* they begin with in their reasoning, their *viewpoint* on particular issues or problems?

6. To what extent are students demonstrating through their portfolios the development of dispositions of mind--for example, to think with *intellectual empathy, intellectual humility, intellectual perseverance, intellectual integrity, intellectual civility?*

These are just some of the questions we would need to ask to determine the quality of the portfolio or alternative assessment.

Likely Misuse: Portfolio assessments can be done well or poorly. Again, as a general rule, when students are asked to write extensively and apply ideas through written work, some learning will take place. All things being equal, then, portfolio assessment is better than traditional assessment. However, portfolios can easily contain written work that is superficial, vague, unclear, inaccurate, narrow, irrelevant, inconsistent, and lacking in insight. For portfolios to be done well, critical thinking must be infused into the learning and teaching process.

Problem Solving

Essential Idea: Students will not be prepared to learn or understand their experience or to respond successfully to new situations if they do not learn to reason well in solving the problems they face in their lives. In this broad and general sense, problem solving is one of the most fundamental goals of education. Everyone faces historical problems, ethical problems, personal problems, social problems, economic problems, problems in relating to others, and problems in figuring out the direction of one's life. Life is filled with problems. Unfortunately, problem solving has often been approached in a relatively narrow way — for example, focusing on specialized kinds of problems (like intellectual puzzles) and, what is more, seeking some fixed set of steps or procedures to follow.

Proper Educational Use: It is important to teach problem solving skills so that students learn to reason well through the problems they will have to face in their lives. Students should be taught intellectual tools they can use to approach problems irrespective of the problem type. To illustrate, one cannot extract problem solving from a host of other interrelated intellectual activities, such as gathering relevant information, drawing reasonable conclusions, making plausible interpretations, analyzing key concepts, identifying questionable assumptions, tracing implications, and reasoning within alternative points of view. Problem solving is not an isolated skill but a by-product of the use of interrelated skills in conjunction with interrelated understandings and insights.

Likely Misuse: It is easy to lose perspective concerning the appropriate meaning of the expression "problem solving", especially since it is often used by technical specialists in a multiplicity of ways. If one does not keep clearly in mind the broad sense of "problem solving," and thus link it with a broad conception of education, one can easily end up fostering a narrow talent or set of skills at the expense of the broad foundational abilities that enable those who have been truly well educated to be successful in solving the diverse problems of their lives. To put this another way, problem solving and critical thinking are, in the last analysis, indistinguishable. Uncritical problem solving is unintelligible; and critical thinking that fails to help us solve our problems is of little use. One cannot solve problems without thinking well and one cannot think well except by learning to think critically about one's thinking.

"Raise the Standards" Movement

Essential Idea: The idea behind the "raise the standards" movement is the perception that schools are enabling students to graduate with very few skills and little knowledge, hence the perceived need to raise graduation standards to a level appropriate to ensure that all graduates have the skills and knowledge essential to successful functioning in the "real" world.

Proper Educational Use: The proper educational use is much more challenging. On the one hand, one must establish across the curriculum universal intellectual standards which ensure an integrated, convergent curriculum focused on deep and essential skills, abilities, understandings, and knowledge. On the other hand, one must establish long-term staff development which enables teachers to grasp the new standards in a substantial way, shift their understanding of the content they are teaching (as a result), and devise new ways to design instruction so that students increasingly use what they are learning in one class to do better work in all of their other classes, and ultimately to reason better in life.

The content taught must be re-conceptualized as modes of thinking-history understood as historical thinking, science as scientific thinking, math as mathematical thinking — and every mode of thinking must be understood as requiring the same essential intellectual standards: clarity, accuracy, precision, relevance, depth, breadth, logicalness, and significance. Students must be taught in such a way that they learn to routinely question their own thinking, whether they are doing scholastic or non-scholastic tasks. Am I being *clear* enough? Am I representing things *accurately*? Do I need to be more *precise*? Am I sticking to the *main question*? Am I dealing with the *complexities* in the task? Do I need to consider another *point of view*? Am I reasoning *logically*?

Likely Misuse: In any "Raise-the-Standards" movement, the danger is twofold:

1. the "wrong" standards may be put in place, and
2. new standards may be imposed but not introduced with other appropriate reforms needed to make those standards accomplish the end intended.

Let us look at each of these dangers in order.

First the danger of the "wrong" standards. The easiest, most superficial, and least useful way to "raise" the standards is simply to "multiply" them, to go through the curriculum and simply add to what we already have: fragmented lower-order skills and "knowledge" easy to test, but which do not produce more highly qualified graduates.

Our "better" students are already adept at cramming for tests, at committing fragmented bits and pieces of content to short-term memory for this purpose. Under ordinary conditions, their skill in studying for short-term recall has little relationship to successful performance later when they enter the job market or when they have to solve problems in everyday life.

This tendency to increase the number of lower order fragmented standards, which are tied to lower order fragmented content, is apparent in much of the movement toward teaching with task-specific "rubrics." We end up with "rubric" filled instruction, with little substance as the payoff, but much superficial assessment along the way.

The second danger is that of establishing substantially higher standards while failing to provide the support system essential to preparing teachers to teach those standards. This is apparent when we merely make a testing program more difficult. The result is twofold. Some teachers learn how to teach to the test in a way that defeats the purpose of the test. In this case, the students become test-wise in the specific tests they are given, even though their performance on the test does not reflect deeply learned new concepts or skills, but merely test preparation skills. Other teachers simply continue to teach in their habitual ways while greater numbers of students fail, become frustrated, and develop lower self-esteem.

Restructuring Schools Movement

Essential Idea: The idea behind the restructuring schools movement is that if schools are to systematically improve, they must change in a systemic way. That is, they must change many major features, if not simultaneously, then almost simultaneously. They must plan for change across virtually all fronts at the same time, understanding how the *structure* of schools as a whole is a function of the structure of the various interrelated parts of that whole. At base, the *system* is usually understood to consist in three things:

1. the ways in which teachers, students, parents, administrators, and community members function in relation to each other,
2. the ways in which they understand their own roles, and
3. the ways in which they conceptualize learning and education.

Proper Educational Use: There can be no question but that schools operate in accordance with the interrelation of various parts of school structure. It is also clear that, for the most part, throughout schooling at all levels, systemic change is needed to create *actual* education communities. There can be no question but that the way teachers, students, parents, administrators, and community members function in relation to each other, the way in which they understand their own roles, and the way in which they conceptualize learning and education are in need of fundamental change. The problem occurs when we move from admitting this "structural" problem to acting on it.

Likely Misuse: Restructuring works only to the extent that teachers, students, parents, administrators, and community members have a sound conception of what produces quality teaching and learning. But changing the actual conception of all these groups is a long-term, challenging project. The conceptions of teaching and learning that people have and use every day are deep-seated and highly resistant to change not only because they are subconscious and automatic, but also because they are long-standing. They have been built up over many years. They are tied into many conceptions that go far beyond schooling. They are products of the way in which people think in general. They translate into behavior without the individual knowing the translation is taking place. It is one thing to "rethink" the routines of schooling. It is another to rethink them in an effective way, so that they are significantly and appropriately modified. To do so requires some insight into way the reform movements of the past have failed. It requires that teachers, students, parents, administrators, and community members learn how to systematically "upgrade" their thinking. *If the way people act is a function of the way they think, then to change action requires a change in thinking.* But if changing our thinking is a matter of long-term, evolutionary growth, then changing the way we act is likewise a function of long-term, evolutionary growth. The question becomes something like this: how can we produce revolutionary changes in school structure by people who need to change their thinking in a long-term, evolutionary way in order to create the change we need?

In some sense, the real problem consists in believing that deep and significant change can occur in a short period of time. We can make large-scale external changes in a short period of time, but not large-scale internal changes. The failure to take the long view, to put things into perspective, and to work effectively in that perspective, is our most pressing problem.

School-Based Management

Essential Idea: The idea behind school-based management initiatives is that reform efforts at individual schools are limited by school district bureaucracies, and that if schools are freed of such restraints, they will be able to successfully initiate real reform.

Proper Educational Use: It is plausible that increased autonomy produced through increased freedom from bureaucratic constraints is likely to produce some change in classroom instruction. However, it in no way guarantees substantive positive change. Change may be change for the worse, or merely cosmetic in nature. For school-based management to be genuinely positive, it is essential that there be genuinely insightful leadership at the school. The principal and at least some of the teachers must be well informed enough to seek long-term objectives, to avoid superficial or empty rhetoric (such as that found in most mission statements), to recognize that the quality of instruction is dependent on the quality of thinking that designs and implements instruction, to grasp that the quality of learning is dependent on the quality of the thinking that produces that learning, and that only a foundational commitment to intellectual standards and critical thinking across the curriculum produces the kind of change that makes a real difference in how students learn and grow.

As Murnane and Levy (1996) put it, both schools and private sector firms have to learn to manage "through a set of five basic ideas — Five Principles — to elicit the front-line effort that improved performance requires...":

- Ensure that all front-line workers understand the problem.
- Design jobs so that all front-line workers have both incentives and opportunities to contribute to solutions.
- Provide all front-line workers with the training needed to pursue solutions effectively.
- Measure progress on a regular basis.
- Persevere and learn from mistakes; there are no magic bullets.

Likely Misuse: School-based management works only to the extent that teachers have a sound understanding of what impedes high quality learning and what needs to be done to cultivate it. However, research conducted by the Center for Critical Thinking (in combination with extensive experience in developing inservices for teachers), strongly implies that very few teachers understand what critical thinking is or how to teach for it.

To spell this out, very few teachers understand intellectual standards or can distinguish them from what are commonly called "rubrics." Few teachers are comfortable with either theoretical questions or abstractions (both of which are essential to the understanding of critical thinking). Very few teachers know how to teach math as mathematical thinking, science as scientific thinking, geography as geographical thinking. Very few teachers know how to integrate ideas within subjects or how to teach students to be effective problem solvers and communicators. The result is that even with the freedom of school-based management, teachers and their local administrators are likely to design systems that produce superficial rather than substantial change.

School Choice

Essential Idea: The idea is that if schools have to compete for students, they will be forced to provide what parents want. And assuming that parents want what is best for their children and can determine when they are getting it, school choice will force the schools to improve.

Proper Educational Use: It is plausible that increased competition between schools for students — assuming the competition to be truly fair — can be one contributing factor to increased quality.

Likely Misuse: However, competition will increase quality only to the extent that parents can articulate a demand for what will actually increase the quality of learning. For example, if parents do not realize that intellectual standards are essential for intellectual growth, they will not ask for them. If parents do not realize that higher paying jobs are connected to high levels of reasoning and problem solving skills, they will not ask for an emphasis on such skills. If parents do not realize that command of language is connected with precision of thought and both are dependent on extended practice in writing that requires command of educated usage and careful word choice, they will not ask for them. If parents do not understand that to master math is to learn to think mathematically, they will not ask for an emphasis on mathematical thinking (or scientific thinking or learning how to think like a good reader, etc.…).

Thus, school choice works only to the extent that parents have a sound understanding of what impedes high quality learning and what is best done to cultivate it. Some years back my son's elementary school sponsored a science fair. I asked him what he was going to do and he said "I will build a kaleidoscope." When I asked him how he was going to do this, he said "My teacher gave me the directions." It turned out that all the students were given a list of possible projects, along with directions. In addition, each student was assigned the task of producing 25 papier mache flowers to decorate the school for the science fair. When I asked my son, "What is science?," he said, "I don't know." When I asked him, "What kinds of problems do you think scientists try to solve?," he said, "I don't know." When I followed up these questions with others about what a hypothesis is, what a theory is, he said, "We don't have to know *that* to be in the science fair." On the day of the science fair the parents were enthralled, with many "oohs" and "ahs" about the huge papier mache dinosaur. It appears that I was the only one who knew that the emperor had no clothes.

School-to-Work Movement

Essential Idea: The essential idea behind the School-to-Work movement is that traditional education does not adequately prepare students for today's workplace. The idea is that "academics alone" (reading, writing, speaking, computation, problem solving, reasoning), though necessary, do not sufficiently prepare students to function well in the world of work they will face. School-to-Work is usually a locally developed, locally controlled initiative that includes collaboration among teachers, administrators, colleges, businesses, and the community to help students attain the knowledge and experience necessary for making informed career decisions and more successfully functioning in the workplace. It often involves work opportunities while students are still in school, and fosters skills that students can use in any job. It attempts to provide the knowledge and experience necessary for making informed career decisions.

School-to-Work programs advocate making learning more relevant by focusing on the connection between educational choices and future career opportunities. School-to-Work programs often purport to help students:

- improve problem solving and critical thinking abilities.
- recognize the need for math, science, and communication skills.
- develop good work habits and show increased "job readiness."
- improve technical skills.
- develop leadership and teamwork skills.
- better understand how to explore career opportunities — identifying their career goals and learning how to reach those goals.
- see the importance of higher education in planning a career.

The premise is that well-designed school-based instruction should prepare students to be effective and desirable employees in the job market upon graduation. To make this process as successful as possible, School-to-Work programs often collaborate with business enterprises. As part of this thrust, there is often greater emphasis on making the classroom function like a job setting, with tasks similar to the tasks and demands of a "working" environment.

The classrooms designed on this model often focus, therefore, on "application" skills, and consider theory only when it directly bears on application. At the same time, because today's job market is increasingly "technological" in nature, with more and more understanding of advanced and sophisticated computer and electronic technology presupposed, there is a large emphasis in School-to-Work programs on technical training, especially in computer systems. School-to-Work enthusiasts focus on business/school partnerships and career analysis, exploration, and planning. Language which occurs frequently in this model include expressions like *contextual learning, applied academics, hands-on laboratories, hands-on learning, workforce trends, workforce preparation, community connections, bridge programs, work-based learning, partnering with business, workplace issues and problems, workplace skills, workplace readiness, technical writing, career education, workplace communication skills,* and *industry analysis.*

Proper Educational Use: It is clearly appropriate and important to assess the proper relationship between school and work. One of the most important goals of schooling is to help those who are schooled become prepared for the world in which they do live and will live, including the world of work. Thus, to the extent that schools do not successfully prepare students for gainful employment upon graduation, they fail in one of their fundamental responsibilities.

Likely Misuse: There are three primary questions we should ask when evaluating a School-to-Work program:

  1. What skills should be fostered to enable students to better function in the world of work?
  2. How do those skills connect with the concept of education?
  3. How will teachers foster these skills?

Clearly decisions have to be made as to which skills sets students should be learning. There is only so much time in the day, many skills to be learned, and teachers have to use their time wisely in the classroom. Therefore they should focus primarily on the skills *most generalizable*, both in terms of learning within every subject and discipline and in functioning well in the workplace. Fortunately, these skill sets overlap. One of the primary abilities employers have increasingly requested and are now demanding, is the *ability of students to think critically*.

Robert Reich (1992) identifies four components of the kind of thinking that highly paid workers will increasingly need to master (pp. 229-233):

1. Command of abstractions: discovering and, when appropriate, controlling patterns, meanings and definitions in thinking
2. Ability to think within systems: to see relationships among ideas, information, disciplines and subjects.
3. Propensity to experiment and figure things out for themselves: to comprehend causes and consequences, to work through complexities and frustrations in working through problems
4. Ability to collaborate: to communicate effectively and work through ideas and problems with others.

All of these components presuppose the ability to think critically, to reason your way through issues and problems skillfully, to reason within multiple viewpoints, to have confidence in your ability to figure things out, to take command of the ideas that are guiding the decisions you make and the way you see things, to see interrelationships between ideas and concepts, data and information. Further, most of these components are necessary for reasoning well within all content. One cannot, for example, learn to think within any subject or discipline without taking command of the abstractions that define the content. In the same way, one cannot learn to think within any subject or discipline without developing the ability to think within the system that is the subject, and without learning the relationships between that system of meanings and other systems of meanings. One cannot learn to think within a subject without learning to "experiment," as Reich calls it, to figure things out within the subject.

Seen in this way, when teachers place critical thinking at the heart of instruction, students not only learn to reason well within the content, but they also, at the same time, learn the skills they will need to function well on the job.

Finally, it is critical to place at the heart of schooling a rich and substantive concept of education so that the needs of business and industry are always secondary to the development of the educated person. Otherwise, the schools can easily become training grounds for whatever business and industry might want, without regard to whether such motives can be connected with education, properly so called. In other words, business needs and concerns *cannot define an educated person.* In 1852, John Henry Newman wrote what has come to be recognized as the best developed treatise ever written on the idea of education. Here is one relevant passage, taken from his book, *The Idea of a University*:

> Truth, of whatever kind, is the proper object of the intellect; its cultivation then lies in fitting it to apprehend and contemplate truth... the intellect in its present state...does not discern truth intuitively, or as a whole. We know, not by a direct and simple vision, not at a glance, but, as it were, by piecemeal and accumulation, by a mental process, by going round an object, by the comparison, the combination, the mutual correction, the continual adaptation, of many partial notions, by the employment, concentration, and joint action of many faculties and exercises of mind (p. 109).

> All this is short of enough; a man may have done it all, yet be lingering in the vestibule of knowledge:--he may not realize what his mouth utters; he may not see with his mental eye what confronts him; he may have no grasp of things as they are; or at least he may have no power at all of advancing one step forward of himself, in consequence of what he has already acquired, no power of discriminating between truth and falsehood, of sifting out the grains of truth from the mass, of arranging things according to their real value (p. 109).

> Such a power is an acquired faculty of judgment, of clearsightedness, of sagacity, of wisdom...and of intellectual self-possession and repose-- qualities which do not come of mere acquirement. The eye of the mind, of which the object is truth, is the work of discipline and habit (p. 109).

> It is education which gives a man a clear conscious view of his own opinions and judgments, a truth in developing them, an eloquence in expressing them, and a force in urging them. It teaches him to see things as they are, to go right to the point, to disentangle a skein of thought, to detect what is sophistical, and to discard what is irrelevant. It prepares him to master any subject with facility (p. 126).

In sum, when teachers foster a rich concept of critical thinking, students will learn the skills, abilities and traits required for functioning as fair-minded thinkers in the workplace. At the same time, *educating the mind* must always be the primary focus of schooling at all levels (never merely serving the interests of business and industry). The question then becomes, *how will we prepare teachers for this complex task?*

Self-Esteem Movement

Essential Idea: If students do not think of themselves as *capable* of performing well in school, they will lack the motivation to try. If they think of themselves as "stupid" or "dumb," this attitude will negatively impact their work. On the other hand, if they have an inflated sense of their capabilities, if they think of themselves as *being smart enough*, they will not be motivated to work hard and strive for high achievement.

Educational Use: It is important to teach in such a way as to encourage students to see themselves as capable of learning to think their way through content and develop important skills of mind. Since most people use only a small percentage of their available intelligence, there is no objective reason for students to think of themselves as incapable. All of us are capable of functioning at a higher level than the level we generally accept in ourselves (even those who think of themselves as "really smart"). The important thing is to accurately assess one's level of ability and continually seek to increase that level, day by day, one step at a time — which is possible largely through the development of *intellectual humility*. When we integrate critical thinking with self-esteem, by teaching students how to accurately assess their strengths and weaknesses, their capacities and potential, we help them develop a *realistic* sense of self, a keen sense of where they are (in their development), where they would like to go, and how to get there. Students develop confidence in reason, in their ability to learn and figure things out for themselves using good reasoning, as they learn to accurately assess their work and see their development in a reasonable perspective.

Likely Misuse: When self-esteem is not properly understood, it easily reduces to mere egocentrism and an improperly *puffed up* sense of self. It is easy to inadvertently encourage intellectual arrogance in students. It is more challenging to help students recognize that they are capable of continual improvement in their thinking and their work, without giving them an inflated sense of what they know or are able to do. When students are encouraged to believe that their work is better than it is, they can't learn how to accurately assess their thinking. They confuse work that is mediocre with high quality work. They come to believe that work which is inferior is just fine, that work which is good is very good. To develop as thinkers, students must be taught that the highest level of self-esteem is that which enables them to *objectively* recognize their weaknesses (without thinking badly of themselves) as well as their strengths and to be always motivated to improve.

Socratic Questioning

Essential Idea: The term *Socratic questioning* has been popular in schooling for a number of years, and typically refers to questioning which opens up an idea and leads to fruitful dialogue, usually between a teacher and one or more students.

Proper Educational Use: *Socratic questioning* should be understood as disciplined questioning that can be used to pursue thought in many directions and for many purposes, including: to explore complex ideas, to get to the truth of things, to open up issues and problems, to uncover assumptions, to analyze concepts, to distinguish what we know from what we don't know, and to follow out logical implications of thought. The key to distinguishing Socratic from other forms of questioning is that Socratic questioning is systematic, disciplined and deep, and usually focuses on foundational concepts, principles, theories, issues or problems.

Socratic questioning is often referred to in teaching, and has gained currency as a concept in education particularly in the past two decades.

Teachers, students, or indeed anyone interested in probing thinking at a deep level can and should construct Socratic questions and engage in Socratic dialogue. When teachers use Socratic questioning in teaching, their purpose may be to probe student thinking; to determine the extent of student knowledge on a given topic, issue or subject; to model Socratic questioning for students; or to help students analyze a concept or line of reasoning. Students should learn the discipline of Socratic questioning so that they begin to use it in reasoning through complex issues, in understanding and assessing the thinking of others, and in following out the implications of what they and others think.

Teachers can use Socratic questioning for at least two purposes:

1. To deeply probe student thinking, to help students begin to distinguish what they know or understand from what they do not know or understand (and to help them develop intellectual humility in the process).

2. To foster students' abilities to ask Socratic questions, to help students acquire the powerful tools of Socratic dialogue, so that they can use these tools in everyday life (in questioning themselves and others). To this end, teachers can model the questioning strategies they want students to emulate and employ. Moreover, teachers need to directly teach students how to construct and ask deep questions. Beyond that, students need practice to improve their questioning abilities.

Socratic questioning illuminates the importance of questioning in learning (indeed Socrates himself thought that questioning was the only defensible form of teaching). It illuminates the difference between systematic and fragmented thinking. It teaches us to dig beneath the surface of our ideas. It teaches us the value of developing questioning minds in cultivating deep learning.

The art of Socratic questioning is intimately connected with critical thinking because the art of questioning is important to excellence of thought. What the word "Socratic" adds to the art of questioning is systematicity, depth, and an abiding interest in assessing the truth or plausibility of things.

Critical thinking and Socratic questioning share a common end. Critical thinking provides the conceptual tools for understanding how the mind functions (in its pursuit of meaning and truth), and Socratic questioning employs those tools in framing questions essential to the pursuit of meaning and truth.

The goal of critical thinking is to establish an additional level to our thinking, a powerful inner voice of reason that monitors, assesses, and reconstitutes, in a more rational direction, our thinking, feeling, and action. Socratic discussion cultivates that inner voice through an explicit focus on self-directed, disciplined questioning.

In *The Art of Socratic Questioning* (Paul and Elder, 2006), we focus on the mechanics of Socratic dialogue, on the conceptual tools that critical thinking brings to Socratic dialogue, and on the importance of questioning in cultivating the disciplined mind.

Likely Misuse: The most common misuse of Socratic questioning is one in which a superficial approach is taken, when no clear principles are offered or used in the questioning process. It happens when questioning is open-ended but not systematic and explicit, when teachers are reaching for tools to improve the questioning process, but are coming up short. The tools of critical thinking are essential to high quality Socratic questioning precisely because they focus on *reasoning*. Critical thinking principles and concepts are necessary for adequately probing, understanding, assessing and improving reasoning. And it is reasoning which Socratic questioning should help improve.

Teaching For Understanding

Essential Idea: The idea behind "teaching for understanding" is the notion that students can "know" (recall) something without having much understanding, and that facilitating student understanding requires teaching that goes beyond the still dominant *lecture mode of teaching* paradigm. One teaches for understanding when one teaches so that students can, for example, explain the concepts they are learning in their own words, find examples of them from their own experience, use them to generate new ideas or solve non-routine problems. Those who advocate a shift to teaching for "understanding" look to design activities so that students must "perform" in ways that demonstrate understanding. They also tend to emphasize the need for ongoing student self- and peer-assessment. For example, one understands "democracy" only when one can evaluate for oneself whether a given set of arrangements is or is not "democratic." Students, in this model, need to argue, discuss, and question their own understandings, as well as relate what they are learning to their lives.

This approach is linked to a *constructivist* approach, a *performance-based* approach, and to *critical thinking*.

Proper Educational Use: It is clear that students who simply rotely memorize bits and pieces of information and formal definitions for tests are not truly acquiring knowledge useful to them. It is clear, in other words, that anyone with a rich concept of education will support the view that we should teach for understanding. There are now available many resources which provide illustrative examples of specific ways in which teaching for understanding might apply to a variety of subjects. Keeping the concept and these examples in the mind's eye in developing curriculum is important.

Likely Misuse: The only danger in a "teaching for understanding" approach occurs when it utilizes a superficial conception of *understanding* and how it can be achieved. This, however, is no small danger. Frequently, teachers unknowingly lack a deep understanding of the subjects they teach. It is a rare teacher who grasps the problem as the following teacher does:

> After I started teaching, I realized that I had learned physics by rote and that I really did not understand all I thought I knew about it. My thinking students asked me questions for which I always had the standard textbook answers, but for the first time it made me start thinking for myself, and I realized that these canned answers were not justified by my own thinking and only confused my students who were showing some ability to think for themselves. To achieve my academic goals I had to memorize the thoughts of others, but I had never learned or been encouraged to learn to think for myself.

Teaching for understanding makes sense, then, only if it is, simultaneously, teaching for critical thinking. Teaching for understanding requires a core organizing perspective that enables one to grasp what understandings, out of an unlimited set of understandings, to emphasize. The most important concepts are those most useful for acquiring further learning, and these are, in the first instance, the concepts that underlie critical thinking (the basic elements and standards of thought). Students studying history should understand the basic logic of history (that it is a story we tell ourselves about the past to make decisions about the present and plans for the future). Students studying social studies should understand it fundamentally as the study of the way groups control the behavior of anyone who belongs to them (through imperatives, permissions, and taboos). Students studying algebra should understand it as "arithmetic with unknowns." Students should "understand" that all subjects represent ways of thinking that emerge from basic concepts (forming, ultimately, systems or networks of understandings).

To elaborate further, all content is logically interdependent. To understand one part of some content requires that we figure out its relation to other parts of that content. For example, we understand what a scientific experiment is only when we understand what a scientific theory is. We understand what a scientific theory is only when we understand what a scientific hypothesis is. We understand what a scientific hypothesis is only when we understand what a scientific prediction is. We understand what a scientific prediction is only when we understand what it is to scientifically test a view. We understand what it is to scientifically test a view only when we understand what a scientific experiment is, etc. etc. etc.

To learn any body of content, therefore, is to figure out (i.e., reason or think through) the connections between the parts of that content.

There is no learning of content without these understandings:

- All content/thinking has been generated by organizing **goals and purposes** (that enable us to share in the pursuit of common ends and projects);

- All content/thinking is guided by the **problems** it defines and solves;

- All content/thinking presupposes the gathering and use of **information** in performance & problem solving;

- All content/thinking requires the making of **inferences** from relevant data or information to interpretative conclusions (thereby rendering the data usable by practitioners as they come to judgments within their respective fields);

- All content/thinking is structured by **concepts** (theoretical constructs) that organize, shape, and direct it;

- All content/ thinking proceeds from **assumptions** or presuppositions from which it logically follows (providing "boundaries" for the field);

- All content/thinking generates **implications** and consequences that enable us to make predictions and test theories, lines of reasoning, and hypotheses;

- All content/thinking defines a frame of reference or **point of view** (which provides practitioners with a logical map of use in considering the "moves" they will make),

---

Only when teachers grasp "teaching for understanding" in this deeper way will they be effective in the process. Otherwise, the understandings they are likely to foster will be helter-skelter, unintegrated, fragmentary understandings--and, therefore, ultimately, superficial understandings.

Thematic Curriculum

Essential Idea: The essential idea is that thematic curriculum, instruction and learning can help get beyond fragmentary curriculum, instruction, and learning. A thematic approach is a holistic approach. It can have either an interdiscipinary or an intradisciplinary orientation. When used in an interdiscipinary way, it attempts to link major concepts within various content areas such as language arts, social studies, and science. Used in an intradisciplinary way, it attempts to focus on understanding and integrating major concepts within a subject.

Proper Educational Use: Conceptualized well, thematic instruction presupposes critical thinking, as critical thinking is required for integrating and deeply learning ideas, within and across domains and disciplines. It is important for teachers to "pre-think" the themes they are entertaining, to assess them for *significance* not only to academic learning but to personal learning as well. For example, a unit on "bunnies" at the primary level in which students counted bunnies, studied their families and food, drew pictures of them, and talked about them as pets would not be a significant use of thematic instruction. A unit on bunnies that focused on the needs of the animal, the ecological systems in which they best function, how they function within that ecosystem along with other plants and animals, how and to what extent they are endangered by human behavior (either domestically or in the wild) would be a more significant approach to understanding bunnies. Similarly, a unit on the rainforest might be developed which enabled children to learn in an integrated way about biology, the environment, the food supply, the culture of certain peoples, global problems, etc. A unit on "interpretations and inferences" would make another excellent thematic unit (humans as meaning-givers). In it, one would give students experiences in interpreting events, pictures, stories, situations, data, graphs, maps, poems, their own behavior, the news, advertisements, etc. Or one could develop a unit on "conflicts in the world" and start with animal conflicts within environmental contexts and then move to human conflicts, (including conflicts within stories, arguments, competition, social conflicts, economic conflicts, and war).

The key to all successful thematic instruction (and hence to the design of thematic curriculum) is that it focus on significant concepts, that it have a clearly defined purpose, that it involve problem solving and reasoning, and that students learn to relate what they are studying to life, while assessing their own thinking in the process.

Likely Misuse: One common danger is when "themes" are chosen that are poorly thought through and fail to integrate significant concepts or understandings. A superficial approach to thematic instruction will undoubtedly lead to superficial learning.

References:

Coffield, F., Moseley, D., Hall, E., Ecclestone, K. (2004). *Learning styles and pedagogy in post-16 learning. A systematic and critical review*. London: Learning and Skills Research Centre.

Curry, L. (1990). One critique of the research on learning styles. *Educational Leadership, 48*, 50-56.

Bradberry, Travis. and Greaves, Jean. (2005). *The Emotional Intelligence Quickbook,* New York: Simon and Schuster.

Goleman, D. (1996). *Emotional Intelligence: why it can matter more than IQ.* London : Bloomsbury.

Hirsch, E.D. (1987). *Cultural Literacy: What Every American Needs to Know.* Boston: Houghton Mifflin.

Murnane, R.J. and Levy, F. (1996). *What General Motors Can Teach U.S. Schools About the Proper Role of Markets in Education Reform*. Phi Delta Kappan.

Newman, J. (1996). *The Idea of a University*. Binghamton, NY: Vail-Ballon Press. (This work was originally composed in 1852.)

Paul, R. and Elder, L. (1996) *The Art of Socratic Questioning.* Dillon Beach: Foundation for Critical Thinking Press. www.criticalthinking.org

Paul, R., Elder, L. and Bartell T. (1997) *California Teacher Preparation for Instruction in Critical Thinking: Research Findings and Policy Recommendations*. California Commission on Teacher Credentialing. Sacramento: Foundation for Critical Thinking Press. www.criticalthinking.org

Reich, R. (1992). *The Work of Nations.* New York: Vintage Books.

Stahl, S. A. (2002). Different strokes for different folks? In L. Abbeduto (Ed.), *Taking sides: Clashing on controversial issues in educational psychology* (pp. 98-107). Guilford, CT, USA: McGraw-Hill.

Sternbert, R. (1997). *Thinking Styles*. Cambridge University Press.

Appendix

This appendix is designed to briefly focus on the conceptual underpinnings of critical thinking, which are resupposed in the analyses presented in this guide.

How to Identify the Structure of a Subject:
The Elements of Thought

The Elements of Thought: There are eight basic structions present in all thinking: Whenever we think, we think for a purpose within point of view based on assumptions leading to implications and consequences. We use ideas and theories to interpret data, facts, and experiences in order to answer questions, solve problems, and resolve issues. In other words, all thinking within a discipline:

- generates purposes
- raises questions
- uses information
- utilizes concepts
- makes inferences
- makes assumptions
- generates implications
- embodies a point of view

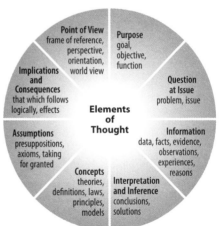

Each of these structures has implications for the others. Change your purpose or agenda, you change your questions and problems. Change your questions and problems, you are forced to seek new information and data. Collect new information and data… For students to learn to think within a discipline, they must become deeply familiar with each of these structions. They should look for these structions as they learn: in lectures, discussions, textbooks, concepts, laws, theories….

For a deeper understanding of these conceptual sets, see Paul, R. and Elder, L. (2006) *Critical Thinking: Tools for Taking Charge of Your Learning and Your Life.*, or The Thinker's Guide Library. www.criticalthinking.org

All Thinking Must be Assessed for Quality Using Universal Intellectual Standards

To evaluate thinking we must understand and apply universal intellectual standards. Reasonable people judge reasoning using these universal standards. When students internalize these standards and routinely use them, their thinking becomes more clear, accurate, precise, relevant, deep, broad, and fair. Note that we focus here on a selection of standards. Among others are credibility, sufficiency, reliability, and practicality.

Clarity:
> understandable, the meaning can be grasped

Accuracy:
> free from errors or distortions, true

Precision:
> exact to the necessary level of detail

Relevance:
> relating to the matter at hand

Depth:
> containing complexities and multiple interrelationships

Breadth:
> encompassing multiple viewpoints

Logic:
> the parts make sense together, no contradictions

Significance:
> focusing on the important, not trivial

Fairness:
> justifiable, not self-serving or one-sided

The Ultimate Goal of Critical Thinking is to Foster the Development of Intellectual Traits or Dispositions

Students need to acquire, not only intellectual abilities (developed through routine application of the intellectual standards to the elements of reasoning), but intellectual dispositions as well. These attributes are essential to excellence of thought. They determine the level of insight and integrity with which persons think.

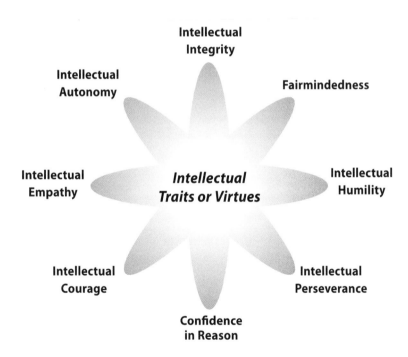

Intellectual
Integrity

Intellectual
Autonomy

Fairmindedness

Intellectual
Empathy

*Intellectual
Traits or Virtues*

Intellectual
Humility

Intellectual
Courage

Intellectual
Perseverance

Confidence
in Reason

Critical Thinkers Routinely Apply the Intellectual Standards to the Elements of Reasoning in Order to Develop Intellectual Traits.

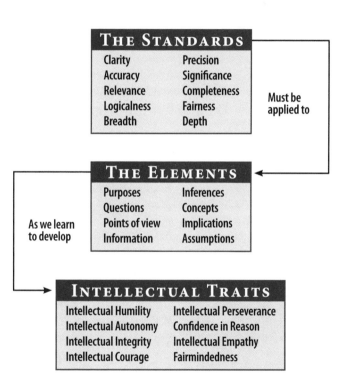

Visit the
Foundation for
Critical Thinking
online

New Resources Available to Online Community Members:

- Critical Thinking Bookstore and Event Registration Desk
- Critical Thinking Forum
- Streaming Video
- Online Critical Thinking Tests
- Online Critical Thinking Learning Tools
- Online Courses for Educators
- Critical Thinking Library
- Critical Thinking New Blogger
- Critical Thinking Resources in Multiple Languages

The
Foundation
for
Critical Thinking

www.criticalthinking.org

The Thinker's Guide Library

The Thinker's Guide series provids convenient, inexpensive, portable references that students and faculty can use to improve the quality of studying, learning, and teaching. Their modest cost enables instructors to require them of all students (in addition to a textbook). Their compactness enables students to keep them at hand whenever they are working in or our of class. Their succinctness serves as a continual reminder of the most basic principles of critical thinking.

For Students & Faculty

 Critical Thinking—The essence of critical thinking concepts and tools distilled into a 22-page pocket-size guide. #520m

 Analytic Thinking—This guide focuses on the intellectual skills that enable one to analyze anything one might think about — questions, problems, disciplines, subjects, etc. It provides the common denominator between all forms of analysis. #595m

 Asking Essential Questions—Introduces the art of asking essential questions. It is best used in conjunction with the Miniature Guide to Critical Thinking and the Thinker's Guide on How to Study and Learn. #580m

 How to Study & Learn—A variety of strategies—both simple and complex—for becoming not just a better student, but also a master student. #530m

 How to Read a Paragraph—This guide provides theory and activities necessary for deep comprehension. Imminently practical for students. #525m

 How to Write a Paragraph—Focuses on the art of substantive writing. How to say something worth saying about something worth saying something about. #535m

 The Human Mind—Designed to give the reader insight into the basic functions of the human mind and to how knowledge of these functions (and their interrelations) can enable one to use one's intellect and emotions more effectively. #570m

 Foundations of Ethical Reasoning—Provides insights into the nature of ethical reasoning, why it is so often flawed, and how to avoid those flaws. It lays out the function of ethics, its main impediments, and its social counterfeits. #585m

 How to Detect Media Bias and Propaganda—Designed to help readers come to recognize bias in their nation's news and to recognize propaganda so that they can reasonably determine what media messages need to be supplemented, counter-balanced or thrown out entirely. It focuses on the internal logic of the news as well as societal influences on the media. #575m

 Scientific Thinking—The essence of scientific thinking concepts and tools. It focuses on the intellectual skills inherent in the well-cultivated scientific thinker. #590m

 Fallacies: The Art of Mental Trickery and Manipulation—Introduces the concept of fallacies and details 44 foul ways to win an argument. #533m

www.criticalthinking.org

Engineering Reasoning—Contains the essence of engineering reasoning concepts and tools. For faculty it provides a shared concept and vocabulary. For students it is a thinking supplement to any textbook for any engineering course. #573m

 Aspiring Thinker's Guide to Critical Thinking—Introduces critical thinking using simplified language (and colorful visuals) for students. It also contains practical instructional strategies for fostering critical thinking. #554m

 Glossary of Critical Thinking Terms & Concepts—Offers a compendium of more than 170 critical thinking terms for faculty and students. #534m

For Faculty

 Active and Cooperative Learning—Provides 27 simple ideas for the improvement of instruction. It lays the foundation for the ideas found in the mini-guide How to Improve Student Learning. #550m

 How to Improve Student Learning—Provides 30 practical ideas for the improvement of instruction based on critical thinking concepts and tools. It cultivates student learning encouraged in the How to Study and Learn mini-guide. #560m

 Critical and Creative Thinking—Focuses on the interrelationship between critical and creative thinking through the essential role of both in learning. #565m

 Intellectual Standards— Explores the criteria for assessing reasoning; illuminates the importance of meeting intellectual standards in every subject and discipline. #593m

 Critical Thinking Competency Standards— Provides a framework for assessing students' critical thinking abilities. #555m

 Socratic Questioning—Focuses on the mechanics of Socratic dialogue, on the conceptual tools that critical thinking brings to Socratic dialogue, and on the importance of questioning in cultivating the disciplined mind. #553m

 Critical Thinking Reading and Writing Test—Assesses the ability of students to use reading and writing as tools for acquiring knowledge. Provides grading rubrics and outlines five levels of close reading and substantive writing. #563m

 Educational Fads— Analyzes and critiques educational trends and fads from a critical thinking perspective, providing the essential idea of each one, its proper educational use, and its likely misuse. #583m

---